LONDON
TRANSPORT
in the 1970s

Michael H. C. Baker

Contents

First published 2006

ISBN (10) 0 7110 3130 4

ISBN (13) 978 0 7110 3130 2

Published by Ian Allan Publishing

an imprint of Ian Allan Publishing Ltd, Hersham, Surrey KT12 4RG

Printed in England by Ian Allan Printing Ltd, Hersham, Surrey KT12 4RG.

Code: 0611/A3

Visit the Ian Allan Publishing website at www.ianallanpublishing.com

Introduction

1 JANUARY 1970 marked the beginning of the end of London Transport as we had known it since 1 July 1933. On that date the 1,267 buses and coaches of the Country Bus & Coach Department passed from the control of 55 Broadway and to that of the National Bus Company — or, to be specific, London Country Bus Services Ltd.

Clement Attlee's Labour Government, to nobody's surprise but not to everyone's delight, had nationalised the railways in 1948, and it seemed inevitable that road transport should go the same way. However, this was a far more complex situation, and although London Transport and the Tilling Group were nationalised at the same time as the railways much of the bus- and coach-manufacturing and operating sector remained outside Government control. To its passengers it was not obvious that London Transport was now Government-owned. There was certainly no suggestion that its familiar red livery should be replaced by Great Western green, the colour chosen for British Railways passenger locomotives, or that the legend 'London Transport' on the side of its vehicles should be replaced by the railways' 'lion on the unicycle' motif. The Conservatives' return to power in 1951 ensured that this was how things would be throughout the next 13 years.

Then, in October 1964, the Labour Party under Harold Wilson, regained control. Just over a year later Barbara Castle, the charismatic, dynamic, red-haired member for Blackburn, in the heart of bus-building Lancashire, was appointed Minister of Transport. She began work on a Transport Policy White Paper, which was presented to Parliament as the 1968 Transport Bill. This proposed that Passenger Transport Authorities would co-ordinate all public transport in the major conurbations, initially Birmingham, Manchester, Liverpool and Newcastle, and that a National Bus Company would take over most other operations. I can remember the vociferous opposition, with slogans demonising Mrs Castle, which appeared all over Merseyside where I was living in 1967/8, travelling regularly on Ribble

(a BET company), Crosville (Transport Holding Co) and Liverpool Corporation buses — all of which would lose their individual identities and liveries. I can't say I was particularly upset by the disappearance of the the uninspiring Tilling green, for this was to be found all over the UK and on both sides of the River Mersey (and was not all that different, come to think of it, from Mersey water itself), and, as it happened, a slight variation of it would become even more widespread once the National Bus Company got going. But imagine the handsome rich blue and cream of Birkenhead Corporation or the gorgeous bright yellow (officially sea green) of neighbouring Wallasey becoming history.

Nevertheless, the Transport Act received Royal Assent on 25 October 1969. Of course, Barbara Castle had advocated her bill with such vigour for reasons rather more profound than the wiping-out of liveries, the chief one being an attempt to stem the hæmorrhaging of passengers away from public transport and into private cars. To this end a New Bus Grant was introduced, a subsidy of 25% on the ex-works price. Only vehicles which met certain criteria would qualify, one of the most important being that they could be one-person-operated, whether single- or double-deck.

OPO was rapidly gaining favour throughout the country as a cost-saving exercise, and implications for London were profound. One of London Transport's biggest costs was, inevitably, salaries and wages. There was little real unemployment in London and the Home Counties, and the unsocial hours demanded of bus crews meant that, unless much more money was on offer than could possibly be afforded, men and women preferred a '9 to 5' (or perhaps an '8 to 4 or 5') working day, Monday to Friday, with weekends their own to do as they pleased. In 1969 London Transport recruited 2,300 new drivers, but 3,000 left. You don't have to be a mathematical genius to realise that this was not good. So if you could dispense with the conductor you could pay the drivers, who now had two jobs to do,

more money and yet still make significant savings. So in 1970 London Transport announced that by 1978 all services would be one-person-operated. Which meant the end not only of the RT (fair enough — the newest would by then be 24 years old) but the entire, much more recent Routemaster fleet. Nevertheless, the RT was still playing a highly significant role in London Transport affairs, there still being no less than 2,775 scheduled for service. Sixty-two of the 69 garages possessed RTs, and, of the seven that did not, Edmonton, Fulwell and Stamford Hill had been trolleybus depots until the 1960s and had never operated RTs.

A new decade and a new company obviously demanded a new symbol, or logo, and so London Country revealed on a bright summer's day its not very bright new image. In later decades all sorts of imaginative logos and liveries would emerge, but 1970 was not a vintage year in this respect. One supposes that the London Country symbol owed something to the classic London Transport one, but it

Above left: By 1970 women were starting to be employed in many more capacities than before within the London Transport organisation, as demonstrated by this lady announcer at Tower Hill Underground station. *London Transport*

Left: Julie Viner, LT's first lady bus driver, climbs aboard RT1608 at Norbiton garage, June 1971. *London Transport*

Above right: MBS302, wearing London Country's short-lived 'Flying Polo' symbol, outside St Albans garage, 14 November 1971. *Hugh Ramsey*

Right: RT4712 on a typically suburban service near Eltham in 1977 — most RTs were to be found operating out in the suburbs by the 1970s.

was much less striking. It consisted of a solid circle encompassed by an open one surrounded by a series of lozenge-like objects which were meant to represent wings; the fact that they looked singularly earth-bound was prophetic — as was the hole in the centre of what was rapidly dubbed 'the flying Polo', representing what had hitherto been known as London Transport's Central Area — for an organisation that was surely doomed to fragment and fall apart.

London Transport had ordered large numbers of AEC Swift single-deckers, shorter by some 2ft 7in than their ill-fated Merlin predecessors, for both Central and Country Area routes, and although London Country would have cancelled the order if it could, it needed new buses; desperate to get rid of expensive conductors as soon as possible, it put 48

Swifts into service in 1970, 90 more following in 1971. Leatherhead was the first garage to receive Swifts, which went to work on routes 418/418A between Kingston and Bookham on 27 June. Given Surrey registrations, the London Country buses were numbered in the same series as the London Transport vehicles. They replaced RTs, a process which would continue, the next being at nearby Addlestone and Guildford garages and, well to the south-east, at Crawley on 1 August. Not only were RTs replaced but also the very last lowbridge RLHs, used chiefly on the 415 and 420 from Guildford and Addlestone garages, were put out of business. The type would continue to operate for London Transport for a further year. The fact that 17 of these 53-seat double-deckers had lasted into London Country days and the era of high-capacity single-deckers was some-

thing of an anachronism. Two of these were from the original 1950 batch, including RLH14, which spent its entire London career at Addlestone garage, passing the factory where its Weymann body was built, several times each day. The RLHs were sold, save RLH44, which was kept for some years as a mobile uniform store, numbered 581J. Four of the 1952 batch, including RLH44, have survived to be preserved.

The first Swifts for London Transport (SM1-10/2, SM11 following a little later) had entered service from Catford on 24 January, taking over routes 160 and 160A. AEC had always called the model the Swift, but London Transport had preferred to label the earlier, longer version the Merlin. The Swift might have been shorter than its Merlin predecessor, but it was still a lot longer than an RT, and diversions had to be found to enable the new buses to negotiate the tight curves on the Middle Park Estate. The SMs should have accommodated 52 passengers, 10 of them standing, but the unions would allow only three, reducing their capacity to 45. More Swifts took up work from Fulwell, Bexleyheath and Hounslow garages on 18 April, whilst in May a group headed northwards to Cricklewood. This completed the delivery of the first 50. These were the only examples to have just one set of doors, at the front; all the rest would be dual-door, although, as we shall see, these were not always used and in some ways simply added to the Swift's problems.

It has to be said that the Swifts were neat-looking, seemingly well-designed buses, both internally and externally, and travelling in one, when it was not full to capacity, was far from an unpleasant experience. No new bus — not even the RT, and certainly not the Routemaster — has ever been totally trouble-free in its early days, and had the Swift not been rushed into service in large numbers and had it not been the 1970s, a period when bus travel was fraught with all sorts of problems, regardless of the quality of the vehicles themselves, then their story might have been different. But history is full of 'if onlys', and the Swift story became a tragedy, not least for AEC, which had had such a long and distinguished association with London. (Indeed, for the best part of 70 years, in most people's perception the London bus was an AEC.) That it should come to such an ignominious end was deeply regrettable.

Meanwhile the last Leyland double-deckers were being withdrawn. A few RTLs and the 6in-wider RTWs were still in use as trainers and staff buses as 1970 opened. They could sometimes be seen keeping company with Merlins and Swifts, for they were distributed widely at garages across London. The end for the RTWs came on 13 June, the final RTLs lasting some three and a half months longer. After this date, although some remained in stock until the spring of 1971, they were delicensed and most were eventually broken up. Earlier withdrawals had been sold for further passenger service, many to Sri Lanka, and a few have lasted to become preserved, although inevitably outnumbered by the more numerous RT class.

Back on the Swift front the first dual-door versions, the SMSs — in by the front door, out by the middle — took up work from New Cross in April 1970 on route 70. However, it was at Edgware two months later that the mixture of poor design, insufficient training and lack of preparation, which was to prove fatal for both Merlins and Swifts, came to the fore, and the proverbial hit the fan. Although passengers were supposed to have the choice of either handing their fare to the driver or using the AFC (automatic fare collection) machines, none of the 32 SMSs had been fitted with full-length ticket rolls and within a short time had run out, and each and every passenger found that he or she had to queue up to pay the driver. One-person operation could never be as efficient as that where conductors operated; it has always only ever been a means of reducing costs in a declining market, at least until modern times, when most passengers have a ticket of one sort or another before they ever get on the bus. No-one had expected the OPO services in the Edgware area to be as fast as in conductor days, but the delays caused by the malfunctioning of the self-service machines and a general unfamiliarity on the part of both drivers and passengers with the new single-deckers dealt the Swift a blow from which it would never recover.

Above: Bromley garage on 14 June 1975. Three generations take it easy on a Sunday afternoon. From left to right, withdrawn SMS318 stands ahead of another unsuccessful Swift with an RM alongside DMS1275, whilst RTs 397, 3490 and 4583, dating from 1947-53, will be out earning their keep yet again on the Monday morning.

Left: An RT and a DMS ease their way through market shoppers and traffic in Beresford Square, Woolwich, in 1978.

• 1 •

Trains and Ships

O N 28 September 1970 the first examples of 212 new cars for the Circle and Hammersmith & City lines took up work. This was the 'C69' stock, visually similar to the Metropolitan Line 'A60'/'A62' stock and rather different from the 'CO'/'CP' stock, some of prewar origin, which it replaced. Built by Metro-Cammell, the 'C69' vehicles were formed into 35 six-car trains, with one spare two-car unit. The 106 motor cars were numbered 5501-5606, the corresponding equal number of trailers 6501-6606. Because of the very different nature of their intended work, compared with the outer-suburban Metropolitan Line trains, the 'C69' cars each had four doors on each side and a consequent reduction in seating to 32. They were neat-looking vehicles, if dull in their unpainted aluminium, and less *avant-garde* than their 'Metadyne' predecessors.

The 'C69s', so called because it had been hoped to get them in service in 1969, were not actually all at work until December 1971. Seventeen trains were required for the Hammersmith & City Line, and 14 for the Circle Line. Decimalisation of the UK currency would take place in 1971, and a similar handshake recognition (rather than embrace) of mainland European practices resulted in the 'C69' stock being measured in metric units as well as feet and inches. The driving motor cars were 16,030mm long (52ft 7in), the trailer cars 14,940mm (49ft), a six-car train measuring exactly 93m. The four traction motors in each driving motor car, manufactured by Brush of Loughborough, were capable of running at 3,800rpm, which translates into a train speed of 60mph, although readers will be unsurprised (and possibly relieved) to learn that it was never intended

Left: A Hammersmith & City Line train of 'C69' stock bound for Hammersmith at Paddington in 1976.

Above: A Shoreditch–New Cross Gate train, with a late-1930s 'Metadyne'-stock driving car leading, at Rotherhithe station.

Above left: The view north at New Cross Gate in 1970. A train of clerestory-roof vehicles on an East London Line working passes the 1930s-vintage Southern Railway signalbox. Beyond are BR Southern Region vans and carriages.

Left: An East London Line train, with a clerestory roof 'K'-stock car of 1927 leading, heads towards New Cross in 1971.

Right: 'G'-stock car No 4248 of 1925 at New Cross Gate in 1970.

The former Humber paddle-steamer *Tattershall Castle* tied up alongside the Embankment, with Hungerford railway bridge prominent and, beyond that, three DMSs crossing Waterloo Bridge, 1972.

that anything like this would be achieved in ordinary service.

The arrival of the 'C69' stock brought to an end the stalwart service of the 'Q' stock, which included the last clerestory carriages in ordinary service in the UK, dating from 1923. I came to know them well in their last days when travelling from New Cross Gate to Whitechapel on the East London Line on my way to lecture at Tower Hamlets FE College, this line being their final haunt. Whether these Underground carriages were the very last clerestories in regular traffic in the whole of the British Isles is a moot point, their only possible rival being No 861, a magnificent Irish 12-wheel brake composite of 1906 which in the early 1970s was still conveying workers the short distance between Dublin's Heuston station and Inchicore Works.

The East End has always been a melting-pot of peoples from many parts of the world, and the early 1970s was no exception, my students ranging from the daughter of the engineer in charge of the locks and lifting bridges in the docks to the son of an Afghan chief. Like the trains which served the area around them, the docks were subject to great changes 1970s; indeed, a mere updating of rolling stock was as nothing compared to the almost total transformation of what we now call Docklands. In the mid-1960s London Docks was handling 93,947,092 tons of merchandise annually, and, as Gordon

Jackson, in his *History and Archaeology of Ports* (World's Work, 1983) noted, 'As late as the early 1970s a trip on the river would reveal a great amount of activity . . . in the port'. Yet as early as 1968 St Katharine's Dock had closed; London Dock went a year later, and by 1979 the Port of London Authority had decided to close the entire docks, leaving Tilbury as the only part still functioning of what a decade or so earlier had been the busiest dock system in the world. To quote Gordon Jackson again, 'The Thames-side wharves . . . suffered dreadfully, with companies going bankrupt, wharves decaying, and workers dispersing . . . [with] unhappy consequences for the local communities'.

The complex network of railways serving the docks withered away. The tramlines had long gone, on the north side by 1940, on the south by 1952; the trolleybus routes, which replaced many of them, were themselves phased out by 1961, and the motor bus reigned supreme. The phœnix-like reinvention into Docklands, accompanied by the revival of rail-borne transport in the shape of the Docklands Light Railway and extensions to the Tube system, lay in the future.

A New Company — Enter London Country

LONDON COUNTRY awoke on 1 January 1970 to find it owned 1,267 buses and coaches. This total comprised 484 RTs, wonderful vehicles but not designed for the world of the 1970s and none dating from later than 1954, 209 Routemasters, rather newer but likewise far away from being fit for the new decade, 413 RFs, single-deck equivalent of the RT (although 175 Green Line versions had been modernised fairly recently), 10 totally outmoded normal-control GSs, 17 equally outmoded lowbridge RLHs, 109 highly unreliable Merlin single-deckers, 14 unreliable Reliance coaches, three Leyland Atlanteans and eight Daimler Fleetlines, the average age of the fleet being 15 years. Anyone foolish enough to suggest that Santa Claus had been generous or even halfway decent seven days earlier would have deserved all the abuse they got; Scrooge would have made a far more appropriate fairy godfather for the new company. London Transport had not helped by failing latterly to invest

in the Country Area, but increasing car use meant that rural services were becoming less and less viable nationwide, and unless the Government, either directly or through local authorities, was prepared to invest unrealistically large sums of money in supporting the rural bus, London Country was going to be a much slimmer set-up by New Year's Day 1980 than it was now.

There was the odd silver lining, and I visited one such spot — Stevenage. Created as a 'new town' after World War 2, it was planned to expand until its population reached 105,000. An earlier 'new town', Crawley, some 60 miles to the south, had been designed without anyone taking into account the extraordinary expansion of private motoring in the late 1950s and '60s, with the result that buses were having an almost impossible job negotiating the rows of cars parked on either side of the narrow residential roads. Stevenage wished to avoid this situation, and in February 1970 a group headed by economics

RML2317 of Godstone garage heads through Redhill on its way from Bromley in the first few weeks of 1970. 'LONDON TRANSPORT' has been painted out, but the name of its new owner has not yet been applied.

Left: RT3430 of Crawley garage at West Croydon bus station in 1971.

Below: GS62, GS10 and an RT leave Chiswick Works on 19 October 1971 on works services. GS10 has a London Country blind but retains its 'LONDON TRANSPORT' fleetname. *Michael Dryhurst*

Right: An official
London Country picture
of Atlantean XA48 posing
for the camera in 1970,
before the application of
the 'Flying Polo' symbol.
If ever a bus could have
done with a bit of
decoration and a few
adverts to brighten up
its inelegant lines,
this is surely it.
*London Country
Bus Services*

Below: MB92 at work
in Crawley *c*1972.
Crawley was the last
London Country garage
to operate the unsuccessful
Merlins, whilst MB92
was the last F-suffix
example in service,
lasting until early 1980.

professor Nathaniel Lichfield put before the public a report estimating that to invest in improvements to the road system to cope with an ever-growing use of the private car would result in repayments of over £200,000 per annum, whilst providing a subsidised bus service would cost only £140,000. Such studies are worthy and need to be done, but such precise costing has to be viewed with extreme scepticism, for people's preferences are notoriously fickle, and all sorts of factors can make such estimates flights of complete fancy.

In order to tempt motorists out of their cars and into buses a service, the 'Blue Arrow', was inaugurated which would run virtually door-to-door between home and workplace during peak hours. It began at the very end of 1969, with the Ministry of Transport covering any operating losses for the year 1970. Three XF-class Daimler Fleetline double-deckers (only two were needed initially, the third being a spare) were painted in a distinctive livery of blue and silver and put on two routes — A1 and A2. Each passenger was allocated his or her own reserved seat, a female courier was present, and the drivers

Above: Park Royal-bodied Daimler Fleetline XF7, newly repainted in blue and silver livery for working the Blue Arrow service in Stevenage. *London Country Bus Services*

Above right: SuperBus SM459 at Stevenage, 2 May 1972. This bus would be sold to Wombwell diesels for scrap in August 1981. *B. E. Speller*

Right: An MS-class Metro-Scania in SuperBus livery at Stevenage bus station in 1977.

were especially selected from the senior ranks at Stevenage garage.

This bold initiative succeeded, the number of season-ticket holders increasing by some 30% within the first 18 months of its operation. Of these bus riders 25% had previously gone to work by car. Various developments followed, and in July 1971 'Superbus' began to operate in Stevenage. Five AEC Swifts and two Metro-Scania single-deckers, painted blue and yellow with a bold 'SB' motif initiated the scheme. Despite some teething problems this too

A less-than-pristine RT3536, of Chelsham garage,
at Farleigh Common on a bleak January day in 1975.

proved popular, to the extent that in less than a year passenger figures went up from around 19,000 per week to 36,000. Subsidies remained necessary, encouraging local initiatives and fine-tuning; the 'Blue Arrow' service faded away, but 'Superbus' prospered, even if the Swifts and Metro-Scanias did not, being replaced by Leyland Nationals and Leyland Atlantean double-deckers. But few people really deserted their cars for good, and a great deal of money had to be spent on Stevenage's road network over the years.

The policy of the National Bus Company was to abandon loss-making rural services. It made this crystal clear by announcing in December 1970 that 83 London Country services would be withdrawn. In some cases local authorities provided subsidies, but the pattern throughout the 1970s was of cutbacks and retrenchment, as it was throughout the NBC empire.

· 3 ·

Shades of Green

THE dark Lincoln green of London Transport's Country Area looked well enough when newly applied and relieved by plenty of white or, even better, the pale green and black of prewar years, but by 1970, when the only relief was a thin cream waistband on double-deckers or window surrounds on single-deckers, it had become all too dull. London Country changed the cream — and the gold fleetnames and fleet numbers — to bright yellow. This ought to have cheered things up a bit, but it just looked rather garish. Then, early in 1972, things got better, the main dark-green colour giving way to a lighter shade. However, this had a very short existence, for at that year's Commercial Motor Show Leyland Atlantean AN90 appeared in an even paler green — leaf green — with a broad white band amidships, grey wheels and NBC-style fleetnames. The Park Royal body itself was of excellent proportions; indeed, it became something of a classic, and the livery suited it very well. The pity was that the National Bus Company's leaf green did not wear well. It was a livery applied to NBC buses throughout

Leatherhead's AN26, with 'flying Polo' London Country symbol, being overtaken by Chelsham's RT3752 at West Croydon, 1973.

19

Above: AN116 of Godstone garage heads south through Caterham-on-the-Hill during 1976.

Below: Delivered in 1971/2 were 90 Park Royal-bodied AEC Reliances for Green Line work. Newly delivered RP13 heads along the Romford ring road (what exotic images that conjures!) in January 1972. *J. Rickard*

RF623 of Reigate garage and AF8 of Godstone garage in Redhill town centre, 1973.

much of England and Wales, so London Country became less and less distinctive, especially as the vehicles it had inherited from London Transport were steadily disposed of throughout the 1970s and replaced by those common to all NBC subsidiaries. Whether this upset its customers, as opposed to enthusiasts, is a moot point; of much more concern was a reliable, comfortable, convenient service. As we move through the 1970s we will see whether this was what they got.

London Country's first new Atlantean, AN1, had arrived in March 1972, the initial batch being completed by the delivery of AN90 in October of that year. They were joined between September and October by another 30, intended originally for Midland Red, this time with broadly similar bodywork by Metro-Cammell. All of the first 120 Atlanteans had LT-type three-piece indicators; they were the last London Country buses to be so equipped. It took a long time for the green and yellow livery to be replaced by standard National colours, the process being not quite complete by the end of the decade.

Unlike London Transport, London Country preferred the Leyland Atlantean to the Daimler Fleetline, although whether this was a wise decision is debatable. However, later versions of the Atlantean were much more reliable than earlier ones and

performed well enough. By the end of 1979 the highest numbered Atlantean in service was AN218, although many more would be acquired in the 1980s, including a number of second-hand examples. However, London Country did receive 11 Fleetlines, with Northern Counties bodywork, in January 1972; another diverted order, this time from Western Welsh, they nevertheless demonstrated London Transport influence in the destination diplay and internal decor. In other respects they broke tradition, for they inaugurated the first double-deck one-man conversion by London Country: sent to Godstone garage, they replaced RMLs on the 410, a route associated first with the very provincial-looking lowbridge Weymann-bodied STLs and then the equally provincial-looking lowbridge RLHs, so in this respect, being essentially provincial buses themselves, the Fleetlines maintained a tradition. Just as it had with its RTs, Godstone kept its RMLs in immaculate condition. Sadly, as the 1970s progressed, standards at Godstone garage deteriorated, not helped, I'm sure, by rumours of closure; one suggestion was that the building would be converted into a sports centre. It did eventually close, being demolished and replaced by a small housing estate.

Above: Close-up of an RML, an AN, an RT and a National at rest inside Godstone garage in 1975. RT986 had been drafted in to help with the vehicle shortage, a revival of a type which had disappeared from this garage some years before.

Below: Godstone garage in May 1976, with XF4, one of the original Daimler Fleetlines of 1965, taking a rest alongside later AN-class Leyland Atlanteans. A Leyland National in Green Line livery can be seen inside the garage.

Above: RT3461, still in LT Lincoln green, about to return to West Croydon from Warlingham Green on a short working of the 403. An RMC, repainted in lighter NBC leaf green, heads north beyond the less-than-graceful trees, January 1975.

Below: Two RCLs at West Croydon in May 1977. RCL2240 has been repainted in the lighter leaf green with NBC-type fleetname and logo, but RCL2246 is still in Lincoln green and has a GY (Grays) garage code. Both buses are working from Chelsham garage on the 403.

Above: West Croydon bus station in the summer of 1977, with, from left to right, Chelsham's RT1018 in NBC leaf-green livery, an early AN-class Atlantean of Leatherhead garage in darker green, an RCL of Reigate garage in leaf green, and a Croydon-allocated DM.

Below: Two new Atlanteans, AN128 of Leatherhead leading, with a Godstone RML behind at West Croydon bus station, March 1978.

• 4 •

Enter the DMS

THE notion that the single-decker could answer most of London's bus requirements had always seemed — to put it politely — odd. The cynics believed that it had been devised by someone who had never endured a journey in such a vehicle during the rush hour, hanging on for dear life by whatever handhold could be reached, trying both to avoid standing on and being stood on by one's neighbour. Had the single-deckers been mechanically reliable and provided with a swift (*sic*) means of getting into the things and then out again, the situation might have been less intolerable. Conductors had been required by law on double-deckers until 1966, but the abolition of this restriction (or asset), the chronic unreliability of the Merlin and Swift high-capacity single-deckers and the relatively satisfactory performance of the experimental XF-class Daimler Fleetline double-deckers paved the way for London's first mass-produced one-person double-decker.

London Transport would have liked such a bus to have been based on FRM1, the rear-engined Routemaster, but the days when an operator, even as large as London Transport, could build (or have built for it) a design to its own specification were gone. The Government's New Bus Grant, of up to 25% of the cost of a new bus, was applicable only to manufacturers' standard vehicles, but AEC, for so long the chief supplier of chassis to London Transport, had become part of the ailing British Leyland and was itself not merely ailing but at death's door, being pushed through it by the disastrous Merlin/Swift misadventure. Chiswick had long since given up building bus bodies, and Park Royal and Weymann, suppliers of most of the RT-family bodies, were experiencing all sorts of troubles. These, like those of AEC, were not unrelated to their geographical position in or close to London, where job opportunities were much greater than in the Midlands or the North. (Which hasn't stopped Dennis, down in affluent, stockbroker-belt Guildford, surviving into the 21st century, but that's another story.)

Ultimately the Daimler Fleetline chassis was chosen. London Transport was still in a position to dictate the body style and specification, and at the

Left: The first of London Transport's standard Daimler Fleetlines, DMS1, is seen in later life at Mitcham while working from Merton garage.

Commercial Motor Show of 1970 at Earl's Court, its new pride and joy, the DMS, was revealed. Two vehicles were displayed, DMS1 and DMS2, and we were informed that, in the tradition of the Routemaster, London's new standard for the decades to come would be known as the 'Londoner'. Unfortunately for Chiswick's (or was it 55 Broadway's?) publicity department Londoners themselves — *i.e.* the people who lived in the capital — were quite happy to wear this title themselves but failed to see why it should grace a big red people-carrier, and despite a press launch at Victoria garage in December 1970

featuring DMS38 plastered with 'The Londoner Bus' posters the name rapidly faded into oblivion. Which, more or less, was also the fate of the bus itself.

Our story is rapidly taking on the gloomy aspect of a Victorian novel in which villains abound, threatening the virtue of the heroine, innocent infants succumb to disease and neglect, and the only relief comes at the very end when we are told that good will triumph in the next world and the wicked will receive their just deserts. Readers may recall that wonderful David Niven film, *A Matter of Life and Death*, where a vast escalator carries the dead up to

Above: DMS46, with appearance-enhancing white upper-deck window surrounds, heads along North End, Croydon's main shopping street, during January 1976.

Right: Seen shortly after delivery in 1971, DMS130, on tram-replacement route 170, leads a fascinating collection of vehicles including an invalid car and a BMC 1100s. The bicycle and the taxi are still familiar sights in Central London today. *V. C. Jones*

heaven, and I've often wondered if its makers, Powell and Pressburger, intended it as a prediction of the London Transport scene 30 years on. There are some very long escalators on the London Tube system, and weary rush-hour travellers must sometimes have hoped that when they reached the top they would find them-selves in a sunlit world where a jovial Cockney conductor, swinging off the handrail of an STL, a 'Feltham' or perhaps a shiny new trolleybus, would welcome them aboard with a cheery 'Hop up, Guv — plenty of seats on top'. However, what they would actually encounter as the decade continued would most likely have been one of the 2,646 DMS-type buses, the last of which entered service in August 1978. Park Royal and MCW built the bodywork, the differences being, as with the RT-family bodies by the same manu-facturers, minuscule. Within the 30ft 10in length 24 seats were provided downstairs, 44 upstairs, and there was standing room for a maximum of 21. The DMS had a very square, upright appearance, but an attractive one nevertheless. It was, in fact, one of the best-looking double-deck designs of its generation. The family resemblance with the Merlins and Swifts, particularly when viewed head-on, was unmistakable.

Two days into 1971 DMSs took up regular work, ousting Brixton RMs from the 95 (Tooting Broadway–Cannon Street) — originally a tram-replacement route — and Shepherd's Bush RMs on the trolleybus-replacement 220 (Harlesden–Tooting). Just why Tooting should be so favoured was never revealed. Another early DMS route was the 5, which passed Tower Hamlets FE College, where I was teaching part-time, and my first ride in one of the new buses emphasised how very different from previous generations of LT double-deckers was the downstairs layout, with its central staircase, two sets of doors and the entrance beside the driver.

Initially the livery was the dullest yet seen — an unrelieved red — although the traditional generous application of posters did much to counteract this.

Throughout their time with London Transport the DMSs were subject to tinkerings with the standard livery, the first variation emerging with DMS76, which was given a white band between decks. DMS118-367 followed suit. Rather more daring — and certainly attractive — was the painting, on DMS46 in 1974, of white upper-deck window sur-rounds. A large group, DM/DMS1968-2646, would be so treated when new in the years 1976-8. One-man-operated, the DMSs (and their crew DM equivalents) had separate entrances and exits, and soon the front doors were being painted bright yellow — well, the surrounds were, not the glass, you understand. Presumably London Transport had such a low opinion of its customers that it feared many of them would have difficulty working out how to get on.

It was at around this time that I attended a lecture at Chiswick Works by a senior London Transport engineer. The DMS was already showing several Achilles heels, and the sad saga of the big OPO double-decker was being played out for all to see. The lecture was fascinating, the lecturer being highly experienced and skilled, and yet I detected an unwillingness to confront the notion that possibly not all the fault lay with the vehicles and that, maybe, some of it lay with LT engineers and, perhaps, some drivers, who were not prepared to adapt to the different world of off-the-shelf buses.

The DMS was fitted with the Gardner 6LXB engine, a powerful 10.45-litre beast that produced 170bhp, greater than anything any previous London bus had been capable of; later examples had Leyland's equally

powerful 11.1-litre 680. Not that such power would prove much of an asset, for DMS-operated routes soon began to lose time. A reduction in vehicle allocation was made on the earliest routes converted to DMS operation, the powers-that-be assuming that the greater capacity of the new buses compared with an RT or an RM would satisfy passengers' needs; however, the type's introduction led not only to a planned-for reduction in frequency but also to much slower boarding times, for, unlike a bus with a conductor, an OPO bus could not re-start until

Seen a few hundred yards from its Croydon home, DMS492 heads for the rural vastness of Chipstead Valley in 1972.

everyone had paid his or her fare. The result was fewer buses, while those that were running were getting further and further behind schedule. No wonder that the DMS almost instantly became unpopular with the travelling public. One could hardly blame the bus, but it beggars belief that London Transport could not have foreseen this. By 1972, belatedly, DMSs were taking over not merely on a one-for-one basis; *more* vehicles than previously were being provided, to make up for the slow-boarding situation.

DMS501 of Merton garage alongside Reigate's RCL2253 at West Croydon in 1975, with a Chelsham RT, another DMS and a Catford RM completing the picture.

• 5 •

Reality Dawns

DESPITE indications that all was not well with the DMS, by the end of 1970 no fewer than 1,967 had been ordered. London Transport was desperate to get rid of the conductor. Yet when the RT finally ended passenger service in 1979, some of the early members of the DMS class had already been withdrawn, the oldest RTs still at work outlasting dead DMSs some 25 years their junior. Variations on the Fleetline engine theme included one of Rolls-Royce manufacture, fitted to DMS864 — schoolboys must have swooned with ecstasy at the notion of travelling to and from school in such a vehicle — whilst Leyland engines were scheduled for DMS1248 onwards. However, these proved horribly noisy, and delivery was suspended until the problem had been alleviated; it was never really solved.

RTs working the 119 and 119A from Bromley garage were in the process of being replaced in 1975, when this picture was taken of an RT and an RM passing in West Wickham.

Back home in Croydon Fleetlines replaced the provincial-type XA-class Leyland Atlanteans on the C1-5 routes serving the vast New Addington estate up on the North Downs, the latter type being withdrawn *en bloc* and sold to Hong Kong. The Croydon Daimlers, DMS1373/6-97, were the first to be fitted with fareboxes. Express services were better than standard, stop-everywhere routes, but New Addington would only get a really satisfactory, high-speed link with Croydon town centre with the advent of Tramlink in the 1990s. Route 10 saw an effort to improve automatic payment by painting right-hand entrance doors on its DMSs yellow, to indicate that this led directly to the farebox, but there was no discernible improvement.

A group of 11 DMSs was allocated to the Round London Sightseeing Tour — an increasingly popular feature of the Central London scene in the summer of 1973. Every six months a new batch of DMSs replaced the earlier one. Inevitably Routemasters,

Top: The front row of a Sunday-afternoon line-up at Catford garage in 1975, a stronghold of the RT until the mid-1970s, featuring two of the class plus a DMS and an RM.

Above: RM161, an early RM without opening upper-deck front windows and a DMS on layover near the Imperial War Museum at Lambeth in 1976. Both are working tram-replacement routes.

Right: Peckham garage in May 1970, with XA28 and RT3722 standing on the forecourt.

Top: A trip to the seaside on summer weekends has been part of the London bus scene for many decades. Two Routemasters are seen parked in Marine Drive, Brighton, in the summer of 1977.

Above: Two rather sad-looking RT trainers stand on the forecourt of the one and only Central London garage at Gillingham Street, Victoria, in 1977.

Left: Transport for London, London Transport and its predecessors have been famous for their posters for the best part of a century. RT549 (HLX 366) displays a poster advertising posters in Sidcup garage, another late stronghold of the RT, in 1977.

Right: Despite being a one-off, rear-engined Routemaster FRM1 remained in service throughout the 1970s, latterly on the Round London Sightseeing Tour, as here in Parliament Square on 28 February 1978.
Julian Bowden-Green

Below right: There was a time when more than 400 trams passed along the Embankment every hour, which quite possibly made it the busiest section of tramline anywhere in the world. Buses were not subject to the same restrictions within the West End faced by the trams, and many of the replacement bus routes were diverted away. One of those which survived into the 1970s was the 109. A Brixton RM is approaching Westminster in 1976.

including the sole rear-engined example, FRM1, eventually displaced the DMSs from this prestigious role.

The most noticeable visual variation on the DMS theme took to the road late in 1977. This was the B20. Its rear end took the form of two massive square air inlets and exhausts, or chimneys. This arrangement was intended to reduce noise and was largely successful, the B20 outliving its predecessors — although this was no great achievement.

It had been intended that all half-cab, open-platform buses, *i.e.* RTs, RMs and RMLs, would be taken off the streets of London by 1978. It soon became obvious that this was a pipe dream and that universal OPO operation in the conditions prevailing in the 1970s would slow down bus travel in Central London to such an extent as to produce virtual gridlock: Utopia would therefore be postponed. The solution would be DMs (without the 'S'), in other words Fleetlines with conductors; therefore 460 DMs were included in the 1974/5 deliveries, and an almost farcical stopgap solution was hastily produced in the shape of 105 standard DMSs complete with AFC equipment but rendered inoperable and signs changed from 'PAY AS YOU ENTER' to 'PAY CONDUCTOR'. One of London's most famous routes, the 16, was the first to employ the DM, followed by the 134 and the 149 at the end of 1974, displacing RMs and RTs.

To quote the 1979 edition of Lawrie Bowles's *London Transport Buses*, 'Late in 1976, London Transport confirmed press reports to the effect that the DMS had not proved a complete success in London service, and it was decided that no more Fleetlines would be ordered after the current deliveries.' Prototypes of one of its successors, the

Above: The final variation of the DMS was the B20. Two 1977 deliveries, DMS2307/15, working from Wandsworth garage, are seen when brand-new at London Bridge.

Below: The B20 featured a revised rear end designed to reduce engine noise, as demonstrated by a newly delivered DMS2476 at Waterloo in August 1977. By this time Fleetlines were badged as Leylands.

Right: Thornton Heath's DM1127 heads northwards through Norbury on 8 January 1979.

Below: Three generations of red buses line up outside Camberwell garage in 1977. Ahead of DMS2189 of 1976 are an RT, an RM and another DMS. The 'Please let the Bus Go First' request would become a nationwide phenomenon on the back of buses, as would the thumbs up sign from a grateful driver if one complied. The patience and good manners of London bus drivers has long been the object of the author's admiration.

vastly more successful Leyland Titan, were already in service, whilst the first of the equally successful MCW Metrobuses would shortly appear.

Overhauls of the DMS class had begun in April 1976, when DMS1 entered Aldenham Works. It emerged a mere 11 months later! Nothing daunted, London Transport began general overhauls, but these took much longer than those of the RT or RM family, it proving impracticable to separate the body from the chassis. Heavier lifting-gear had also to be installed to cope with the cumbersome monster, and eventually London Transport admitted defeat; in 1978 it settled for two-year recertifications without overhaul, and began to get rid of the DMS. It is probably true to say that this also heralded the beginning of the end for Aldenham Works.

Above: Brand new DMS2295 of Brixton garage, seen outside the Croydon Town Hall terminus of route 50 early in 1978.

Below: In 1977, specifically for the Round London Sightseeing Tour, London Transport acquired from Bournemouth Transport seven Daimler Fleetlines with Weymann bodywork convertible to open-top. DMO3 is seen near King's Cross in 1979 . *G. K. Gillberry*

· 6 ·

Bristol Buses Prove Popular

ALTHOUGH no Bristols had been bought new by London Transport since the austere days of World War 2 and its immediate aftermath, there was little surprise when London Country placed an order for LHS midibuses in 1972. Eastern Coach Works-bodied Bristols had been the staple diet of the Tilling companies since before nationalisation, so it was inevitable that London Country would join the club. What was a lot more surprising was that London Transport should follow suit.

Twenty-three 35-seat LHSs, the BLs, fitted with ECW bodies painted in NBC livery, joined the London Country fleet in the summer and early autumn of 1973; they were sent to Dunton Green, St Albans and Amersham garages. Eight-feet wide, they were somewhat oddly proportioned, stubby-looking vehicles. Rather better were their successors, the 7ft 6in-wide

BNs, the first of which arrived in the latter part of 1974. Initially there were 30, intended to work the many rural routes which hitherto had been the preserve of RFs, or, somewhat earlier, the GSs. How lightly trafficked were these routes and how few buses were needed to operate them (sometimes only one or two) is illustrated by the fact that they were spread amongst six garages — Guildford, Dorking, Leatherhead, Chelsham, Northfleet and Hertford. This allocation did not remain for long as patronage continued to fall. Although another 14 BNs arrived in 1977, the LHS proved the exception to the rule that the Bristol/ ECW combination, if not as sophisticated as Chiswick-designed products, was well engineered, long-lived and popular. As the certificates of fitness of the BLs began to run out in the summer of 1980, so the class was withdrawn after less than seven years' service.

Left: One of the 23 Bristol LHS/ECW buses delivered to London Country in the latter half of 1973, BL7 negotiates St Peter's Street, St Albans, on 24 October 1973. *John Gowers*

Above: BN52 takes on pupils from Limpsfield primary school, situated opposite Limpsfied Common on the A25 at the top of the climb from Oxted, in the spring of 1977.

Right: If you go down to the woods today beware of lurking Bristols. BN52 of Chelsham garage stands deep in the Weald at Staffhurst Wood, close to the Surrey/Kent border, in the spring of 1976. Delivered in late 1974, this and two similar buses replaced RFs on a route which had once been worked by GSs.

Left: BN57, one of the 1977 deliveries to Leatherhead garage, working the Epsom town service in the summer of 1977.

Above: Golders Green, on 19 April 1977. FS5, a 16-seat Strachans-bodied Ford Transit based at Finchley, is working the Hampstead Garden Suburb H2 service, whilst RS5, a recently delivered AEC Reliance/Plaxton Supreme 49-seat coach of St Albans garage, is on the 717.

Left: BS15 heads through Brixton on the P4, a route taken over from the FS 'bread vans' in late 1976. Lasting just under five years with London Transport, this very small class of 17 very small buses was snapped up by operators as far apart as the Isles of Scilly and Scotland.

Right: A very short bus. BS9, a Bristol LHS6L with 26-seat ECW bodywork, at Bromley garage shortly before being replaced by the larger BL class in April 1978.

Like London Country, London Transport turned to the LHS to replace the RF. But before we get on to that topic we must note the introduction of the 'bread vans' — Fort Transit minibuses with 16-seat Strachans bodies. Supported financially by the Greater London Council and set to work on local suburban routes in residential areas where there was restricted access, they entered service in 1972. Initially there were 16 (FS1-16), but, these having proved successful, another five arrived in 1973/5, whilst a further five took up work in 1979, replacing five of the originals, this type of minibus usually having a pretty short working life. They were replaced on most routes by Bristol/ECW LHSs, 17 of these 26-seat buses, the BS class, arriving in 1975/6. These would also have short lives with London Transport, all being sold by the end of 1981, although, like so many London buses of this period, they would see further service elsewhere.

A Hants & Dorset Bristol LH, longer than the LHS, was evaluated at Chiswick in 1973, evoking memories of an earlier era when brand-new Hants & Dorset K-type double-deckers had been allocated to London Transport to cover shortages in the late 1940s. The LH was deemed satisfactory, and as a consequence 95 similar buses, constituting the BL class, were ordered. They were fitted with 7ft 6in-wide, 30ft-long ECW bodies seating 39. The BL class proved a good deal more popular with its owner than did its green Country cousins, reversing the usual state of affairs and lending some credence to the notion that LT needed to learn new ways of dealing with off-the-peg buses — and was perhaps doing so; BLs were to survive on passenger duties with LT into the first few days of the 1990s.

Below: BL93, a 39-seat big brother of the BS class, allocated to Uxbridge, stands at the Hillingdon Hospital terminus of route 128. Having commenced work in September 1977, it is seen a short while later adorned in a red and yellow (rather than red and white) livery and with a fairly discreet indication of its sphere of operation but no sign of ownership. *J. G. S. Smith*

National Rejoicing?

THROUGHOUT the 1970s London Transport was forced, kicking and screaming and hanging on to its RFs, RTs and RMs like a small child with a comfort blanket, towards buying completely off-the-peg buses, identical in all but the most insignificant details to those found the length and breadth of the UK. The single-decker which finally confirmed that this was to be the future and that London Transport had better come to terms with it was the Leyland National. Even now, well over 30 years since the first example entered service, in Cumberland as it happened, opinions on whether it was a good, bad or indifferent bus are still strongly held. Leyland's publicity department declared that the National was 'designed like an aircraft, built like a car', which left it wide open to such ripostes as: 'Why don't you design and build it like a bus?' But the Leyland philosophy in the 1970s was dominated by the motor-car side of the business. This had certain advantages — much research had gone into making the private car better able to sustain accident damage and protect the passengers, and the National was immensely strong. Also, being built on a production line with very few variations from the standard, it had little need for skilled labour, and the bus could be built much more quickly than hitherto. But operators had always demanded — and got — variations from the standard, and some aspects of car design and production were simply not suitable for buses.

The Omnibus Magazine of November/December 1970 got very excited about the National. This is what it wrote, referring to the 'tremendous advances represented inside the hall [at Earl's Court] at the Commercial Show . . . there can be no doubt that a bus like the National is long overdue in Britain . . .' London Transport Chairman Sir Richard Way told *The Sunday Times* that he thought it 'quite the smoothest bus ride I've ever had'.

Left: London Country Leyland National LN15 shortly after delivery but before entering passenger service, seen parked at Chelsham garage on a gloomy afternoon in December 1972, with a refurbished Green Line RF in the foreground.

Above: LNC41 stands at the Chelsham terminus of route 706 in the spring of 1973, shortly after delivery. As delivery of Nationals for Green Line service had only just begun they found themselves operating for a while alongside RFs, such as RF121 seen here.

During World War 2 most communities were provided with a National Restaurant, which provided basic, sustaining, not very exciting food at an affordable price. Ours at Thornton Heath Pond was next door to the tram depot, since you ask. I sometimes wondered if the people responsible for National Restaurants also designed the National bus — if you see what I mean. Between 1939 and 1945 we were also provided with ENSA — an organisation which sent entertainers all over the country, and again there seemed to be a connection, for the entertainers varied greatly in quality, even if they had plenty of enthusiasm. Some would have lasted less than a week in peacetime, and there were bus companies (Southern Vectis being one example)

which took a similar line with the National, buying it only because nothing else was available. No-one in Ireland, whether in the Republic or the Six Counties, would have anything to do with the National other than the port of Rosslare, Dublin Airport and County Cork Library Service, which stuffed one full of books and toured it around the more remote districts. London Transport, however, took enthusiastically to the National, which from the start was clearly much more satisfactory than the Merlin or the Swift, whilst London Country was so enamoured of it that it bought more than any other operator in the whole wide world, having no fewer than 540 in service by the summer of 1980.

Left: SNC85, one of the shorter 10.3m vehicles, ahead of a 'modernised' RF outside Hemel Hempstead garage. A company which appeared to have something of a death-wish at this time, Leyland refused to replace the PVC-covered seats on these buses — for that, essentially, is what they were — so London Country carried out the work itself using London Transport-style blue and green moquette before placing them in service between December 1973 and April 1974.

Below: Later SNCs were fitted with high-backed seats more suited to their intended work. SNC200 is seen when new in 1976 at South Croydon, ahead of a DMS working a New Addington express service.

Above: An SNC with ideas rather above its station attempts to give a Daimler saloon a run for its money on the A22 Caterham by-pass in the summer of 1974.

Below: SNB383 of Leatherhead garage at Kingston on 16 March 1979, having been delivered earlier that year. This bus had seats for 41 passengers with standing room for a further 19.

Above: London Transport's first Leyland National, LS1, heads for Clapton Pond on route S2 on 13 August 1973. Behind is one of the Metro-Scanias against which the first six Nationals were evaluated. *E. B. Simpson*

Below: Looking very spruce with its white roof, Metro-Scania MS6 pauses at Clapton Pond on 13 August 1973, its first day of operation. *E. B. Simpson*

London Transport was not far behind London Country in its affection for the National. The first arrived in 1973, and the class would eventually total 506, this figure being reached in 1981.

London Transport's first experience of the National was with an experimental vehicle, delivered in 1973 and used for tests before being returned to Leyland. Later that year the first six to enter passenger service, LS1-6, modified in the light of the earlier vehicle, took up work from Dalston garage on route S2. Despite the manufacturer's insistence that there should be no straying from the Workington commissar's *diktat*, on pain of being banished to Siberia, a standard LT cab door and a rear route-number box were fitted. Given London's traditional generosity in telling prospective passengers (or those that had just missed it) where the bus was going, this latter feature was no surprise. The first Nationals were in the nature of a tentative toe-dip in the water, for they were in competition with six Metro-Scanias. All 12 buses were painted in an attractive livery of traditional red with white roofs. The air-conditioning pod, perhaps the most distinguishing feature of the National, mounted at the rear on the roof, was painted grey. The Metro-Scanias, MS1-6, were distinctive and attractive vehicles, with some rather dashing chrome strips and a very deep nearside section to the

windscreen. However, like so many London buses of the time, they had short lives in the capital, being taken out of service in the summer of 1976 and replaced by none other than SMSs — what a disgrace! However, foreign parts were perfectly happy to make their acquaintance, and five of them headed across the Severn Bridge and were put to work alongside other Metro-Scanias with Newport Transport.

The 'abroad' connection does not end there, for the next Nationals to enter London Transport service were 51 buses originally intended for Venezuela. Merlins and Swifts were now failing in Black Death proportions, and early in 1976 all 51 Nationals plus the six originals were sent to Hounslow, where the distinctive scream of their engines did their best (but failed) to drown out the roar of 'jumbo jets' a few hundred feet above them. Most of the Nationals seated 36, with 27 standees, and by the end of the 1970s they had replaced — or were in the process of replacing — not only Merlins and Swifts but also the last of the RFs, as well as DMSs.

Below: Enjoying a climate somewhat more temperate than that of its originally intended South American home, LS47 proves popular with Hounslow residents on its way southwards to that longtime single-deck haven of Kingston. *M. S. Curtis*

· 8 ·

Steaming Away
and Updating the Circle

IT is a rather extraordinary fact that steam lasted longer on the London Underground than it did on British Rail. Probably very few London Underground passengers were aware of this, but it is nevertheless true that until 6 June 1971, if they had known where to look, they could have seen a former GWR pannier tank going about its legitimate business in charge of an engineers' train.

In 1933 London Transport had inherited a varied collection of steam locomotives from the Metropolitan and District railways. By the late 1950s those that remained were very elderly but were still needed, being employed on engineering duties. The Swindon-designed pannier tank was seen as an ideal replacement, and in October 1956 No 7711 was transferred to LT, repainted maroon and

renumbered L90. Others followed over the years. When steam ended on British Rail in the summer of 1968 seven of the London Transport pannier tanks were still at work. Three survived into the 1970s, and when the time came to withdraw these, in the summer of 1971, such was the interest that a ceremonial run was organised from the Barbican in the heart of the City of London to the Metropolitan depot at Neasden, on 6 June. L94, the former 7752, was given the honour of hauling the train of engineers' wagons, and large crowds gathered at every vantage-point to watch its passing. It then passed into preservation at Tyseley along with L90 (not the original locomotive to carry this number but a later replacement), whilst the third survivor, L95, went to the Severn Valley Railway.

Neasden depot at noon on a Saturday in May 1970, with an ex-GWR '57xx' pannier tank simmering away, having just worked in on an engineers' train.

London Transport, quite correctly, anticipated that there would be much interest when steam finally ceased on the Underground. The crowds certainly turned out on 7 June 1971 to watch the ceremonial last train hauled by pannier tank L94, built for the GWR in 1930. It is seen here approaching and then passing through Finchley Road. A Bakerloo Line tube train of 1938 stock has also managed to steal some of the limelight.

Meanwhile the 'C69' stock had entered service on the Circle and Hammersmith lines, over which pannier tanks regularly hauled their engineers' trains when the commuters were tucked up safely in bed. Whilst not as ground-breaking as the trains of the late 1930s, the 'C69' stock is still in service 35 years after its introduction and has proved a very sound investment.

One of the curiosities of the Circle Line is that because the trains spend all their time going round and round like a very large trainset the wheels wear more on one side than the other. To counteract this each day one train takes itself off the Circle to Whitechapel, from where it reverses back onto the Circle at Liverpool Street and continues on its merry way, now facing the opposite direction. That way all the seven trains in each direction which are needed to operate the 52$\frac{1}{2}$min journey around the Circle, at eight-minute intervals, get sorted.

The 'CO'/'CP' stock of late prewar and early postwar design, which the 'C69' trains replaced, was cascaded to the District Line. This meant that most of the remaining 'Q' stock, which dated back to 1923, could be withdrawn and scrapped. The last of the 'Q's, the only clerestory-roof carriages still in ordinary service in England, survived on the East London Line into 1971. At this time I used to travel once a week from Oxted to Whitechapel, which meant I often found myself at New Cross Gate changing from a Southern Electric '4-EPB' — nominally a lot more modern than the rake of 'Q' stock waiting across the platform but in reality just as rough riding. Not that I minded; I knew time was fast running out, and I rather took delight as we bounced past the Southern sidings and dived down beneath the Thames through the Brunels' (father and son) historic Thames Tunnel to emerge into perhaps the most cosmopolitan area in all London.

Although continuing to serve as a useful link between British Rail-operated surface lines north and south of the Thames, the East London Line, which ran from two termini south of the river, at New Cross and New Cross Gate, to Whitechapel, was much less busy than it had once been, and a general decline in passenger numbers on the Underground system led to the scrapping of a good few carriages of 'CO'/'CP' stock. Five-car sets of these, based far to the west at Ealing Common, worked the East London Line until they were replaced by redundant 1938 Tube stock in January 1974 — a move which went down like a lead balloon with regular travellers. Fortunately by June 1977 further service cutbacks elsewhere enabled the drafting in of four-car units of Metropolitan 'A' stock. During the rush hours the service was extended from Whitechapel to Shoreditch.

Left: A Circle Line train of 'C69' stock pulls out of Farringdon station in the summer of 1976.

Right: An East London Line train of 'G' stock dating from 1923 rattles its way towards Brunel's celebrated Thames Tunnel and its Shoreditch terminus in 1970.

Below: A train of 'C77' stock, newly into service in 1978, seen at Farringdon on a Circle Line working.

• 9 •

Bad News

TRAVELLING beneath the streets of London, whether by near-surface Circle, Metropolitan or District train or much deeper down in the Tube, is remarkably safe. But when an accident does happen the horror, in the dark, hot, subterranean confines is almost beyond imagining. Such was the scene at Moorgate Northern Line station in the morning rush on 28 February 1975. For some reason never determined the 08.37 train from Drayton Park, instead of coming to a halt at this, its destination, appeared to speed up as it drew alongside the platform, ploughed through the sand barrier and smashed into the brick wall at the end of the tunnel at 30mph. Forty-three people, including the driver, died.

One of the survivors in the front carriage, where most of the fatalities occurred, Javier Gonzalez, described what happened: 'The train was not very busy,' (the newspapers, of course, and even the BBC referred to the train as being 'packed'), 'and because I knew the exit at Moorgate was close to the front of the train I got into the front carriage and found myself a seat next to the second set of doors . . . Nothing was wrong until the train shuddered and I leant a little forward, because of the movement of the train. Just above my newspaper I saw a lady sitting opposite me and then the lights went out. I have the image of her face to this day. She died.

'I had been knocked unconscious and have no further memory until I heard a shout in the distance: "Is there anybody there? Can you move?" I had my hands near my shoulders and I tried to lift myself up, but I could not because of pain. I was not fully conscious, did not know where I was, but I shouted back: "No, I cannot move."

'I then heard the distant voice again: "Cover your face up and we'll get you out!" The next thing I remember is that someone was lifting my body, holding me from under my armpits, and I asked him: "Who are you?"

'He said "I am David — I work for the rescue services," so I said: "Thank you, David".' Javier Gonzalez was taken to St Bartholomew's Hospital where he spent several weeks recovering from his injuries.

The rescuers worked in almost indescribable conditions, in temperatures of up to 120°F. The cause of the accident was never established. The driver, Leslie Newson, was in good health, had not taken alcohol or drugs, was 'considered an unlikely suicide candidate' and was known to be 'a careful and conscientious driver'. The brakes were never applied, and the driver had not even raised his hands to protect his face at the moment of impact.

No other event on London Transport during the 1970s could compare, thank goodness, in terms of loss of life, injuries or shock, but in terms of cost, failed hopes and bad publicity there were plenty of other nasty happenings. Perhaps the greatest was the failure of the Merlin and Swift single-deck buses. Too long, unpopular with drivers, difficult to overhaul, with a myriad of unreliable parts affecting the body, chassis and engines, production examples of MB, MBS and MBA Merlins were subject to wholesale withdrawal from 1974, only six years after the class had entered service. By the end of 1975 no fewer than 350 had taken up residence at Radlett Aerodrome awaiting disposal. The entire class had ceased work by the end of 1976, with the exception of those employed on Red Arrow services, which lasted until replaced by Leyland Nationals in April 1981.

London Country fared no better, its final MBSs finishing work in late 1980. Many from both the London Transport and the London Country fleets went straight for scrap, but a good few did find further owners, mostly far away. Around 120 went to Northern Ireland, where I came across them in Belfast and Londonderry and elsewhere in the Six Counties, some still in LT livery, others repainted by Citybus (Belfast) and Ulsterbus. A good few were damaged or destroyed during the 'Troubles'.

In 1976 came the first withdrawals of the Merlin's successors, the Swifts, just four years after the last of the total of 838 — for both London Transport and

Above: In September 1972 a Red Arrow Merlin re-entered service in an experimental livery with white window surrounds which improved an already handsome design. Sadly 'handsome is as handsome does' did not in this case hold true. An immaculate MBA588 is seen at Victoria. *Tom Maddocks*

Below: MBS4 in Epsom whilst working from Leatherhead garage towards the end of its London Country career. One of the prototypes of 1966, it had been transferred to London Country in 1973 and would be withdrawn in December 1978.

Left: MBS409 heads through typical Slough scenery, previously 'celebrated' by John Betjeman and later by Ricky Gervais, c1971. *Ian Allan Library*

Below: London Country MBS431, working a local St Albans-area service, is pursued by a London Transport DMS on route 84 from Potters Bar garage in the summer of 1972. St Albans was the northernmost point normally reached by red buses.

Right: The terminus of route 200 beside the cricket green at Mitcham is one of suburbia's most pleasant spots, with cottages and houses dating back to mediæval times. Batsmen gaining and departing the crease have to negotiate a road in front of the pavilion, a practice which was going on long before the advent of the Swifts and which has long outlasted them. SMS369 of Merton is seen on a summer's evening in July 1977, shortly before DMSs took over the route. This bus would do rather better than most of its fellows, departing for pastures even more pleasant than Mitcham, being sold in 1981 to Pardes House School, Hampstead, and survives today in preservation.

London Country — had been delivered. The type had proved just as troublesome as the Merlin, sharing a lot of the latter's faults and contributing others of its own. London Transport announced that OPO slowed traffic in Central London to an unacceptable degree, and the Routemaster would be needed for the foreseeable future. Overhauls of Swifts ceased in April 1977, orders were placed for more Nationals, and the Swift rapidly disappeared from the streets of London, the last examples, as with the Merlins, being in the Red Arrow fleet, which succumbed to the all-conquering National in July 1981.

Right: Two Swifts, two RMs and two DMSs make a mathematically pleasing (if not operationally so) line-up on the forecourt of Thornton Heath garage. The Swifts, used on routes 115 and 289, outlasted many of their fellows, but all had gone by November 1978, this picture being taken shortly before that date. It is ironic to think that many of the trams once based here here served London for nigh on 50 years.

Right: A very sorry-looking Swift slowly disappears into the undergrowth at the back of Norbiton garage in January 1978.

Above: Swanley garage on a Sunday in May 1975, with SM488 outside and two friends taking a rest inside.

Left: The SMW class comprised 15 AEC Swifts delivered to South Wales Transport between September 1969 and March 1971 but almost immediately exiled to England. One of the Marshall-bodied examples, SMW5, is seen in its new home of St Albans, 14 November 1971. *Hugh Ramsey*

Left: SMA13, one of the 45-seat Alexander-bodied Swifts intended for South Wales but delivered to London Country early in 1972, seen on the duties for which the class was best known, the southern orbital Green Line 725. *Ian Allan Library*

London Country had received 138 LT-type Swifts, the SM class, in 1970/1. Painting them green did nothing to improve their reliability, and although withdrawals started two years later than those of the red buses, by early 1981 they had all gone. London Country also had other Swifts — 15 SMWs and 21 SMAs. The former were ex-South Wales Transport buses, three with dual-door Willowbrook bodywork, the rest having Marshall bodies of typical BET design. The SMAs had also been intended for South Wales but were diverted new to London Country. They had single-door Alexander bodies with coach-type seats and spent most of their lives on Green Line routes 725/726. No more successful than the SMs, all had been withdrawn by December 1980.

The DMS had in some senses an even more dismal record than did the Merlin and the Swift. At least with the single-deckers there was a semi-decent interval between the last deliveries and the first withdrawals, but with the double-deckers these occurred more or less simultaneously, in the summer of 1978; indeed, the last RTs and RFs outlasted some of the Fleetlines. Maintenance problems were escalating, overhaul proved both long-winded and expensive and, like the Merlins and Swifts, some DMSs went straight to the scrapyard, whilst many were sold to other operators; it is worth noting that, unlike the Merlins and Swifts, a significant number of ex-London Fleetlines were bought by front-line operators, which got good value from them. They could, for instance, be seen working hard through the streets of Birmingham, Manchester and Glasgow as well as in many smaller cities and towns — which

suggests that perhaps not everyone considered them an unmitigated disaster. In dwindling numbers they would stayed on in London throughout the 1980s, not finally ceasing normal passenger service until 1993.

An event way outside London Transport's control was the huge increase in oil prices which occurred in late 1973 and during 1974. A number of Arab nations, angered by the West's support of Israel, first held back oil supplies and then savagely hiked prices so that in less than a year they increased fourfold. 'Did this result in drivers' giving up their cars in favour of public transport?', I hear you ask. It did not; well . . . there was a brief period of abstinence before the compulsion to get back behind the wheel became overwhelming, and before the year was out the graph of car usage resumed its inexorable climb, congestion likewise. The GLC attempted to keep fares down and was quite prepared to put in large sums of public money in the form of subsidy to achieve this, but such a policy had its limits, and in 1975 fares, which had been kept steady since 1972, rose by 56%.

An event which could have caused massive confusion and delay was decimalisation, the conversion from pounds, shillings and pence to the one-hundred-penny-pound. In the event its arrival on 21 February 1971 went through remarkably smoothly, chiefly because the Government, local authorities and London Transport and London Country had prepared for it with commendable thoroughness. Ten RTs, fitted out by London Transport as mobile classrooms, which toured the system from September 1970 to March 1971, did much to aid the process.

Right: Most of London's Fleetlines would see further service, either in the UK or overseas, but others were less fortunate. Viewed from another of the class in Ensign's yard at Purfleet, DMS354 awaits its fate. *Ian Cowley*

· **10** ·

Multi-coloured Routemasters

IN 1977 HM The Queen celebrated her Silver Jubilee, and to mark the occasion London Transport turned out 25 RMs in appropriate livery. Sponsors were sought, and for £10,000 you could have your product featured inside and out for seven months. Temporarily renumbered SRM1-25, the buses entered service on 11 April and continued thus until November. They looked absolutely splendid. In addition the wool industry decided this would be a good opportunity to try out the wearing qualities of its products, and each silver-liveried bus was fitted with carpets on both decks. Working mostly in Central London and in particular along

Oxford Street, they made a real contribution to the celebrations.

Two years later we arrived at the 150th anniversary of London's first omnibus, run by George Shillibeer. Fired by the Silver Jubilee success LT turned out 12 Routemasters in a livery of green, cream and red approximating to that worn by the original horse bus. If not quite as startling as all-over silver it was nevertheless very attractive. One further Routemaster, RCL2221, which had been converted into an exhibition and cinema bus, wore this livery. The same year saw yet another special livery, the red and yellow of 'Shoplinker'. This had nothing to do with anniversaries, being a GLC-inspired initiative, a circular service linking the principal West End shops. Sixteen RMs took part this time. Launched in April, the service was not a success and was curtailed in September.

Acton's SRM18 (RM1906) heads across a surprisingly empty Portobello Road. The SRMs were allocated to 21 routes, most (though not all) serving Central London.

Above: Twelve Routemasters celebrated the 150th anniversary of London's first omnibus, operated by George Shilibeer in 1829. RM2153 pauses on a wet evening in Oxford Street on 16 March 1979.

Below, left and right: The newest Fleetline, DM2646, was also adorned in this most pleasing livery of dark green and cream and is seen here at Hyde Park Corner on route 16.

Above left: Immaculate in Shoplinker livery and advertising Austin Reed, RM2154 stands at Hyde Park Corner on 7 April 1979. *Gerald Mead*

Left: One-time London Country RML2319 meets its fate at Wombwell Diesels, 28 February 1978. Parts salvaged passed to London Transport. *Roger Rettig*

Above: Upon return to London Transport ownership one-time Green Line coach RCL2253, in common with the majority of its type, was used initially as a driver trainer, still in NBC leaf-green livery. *G. K. Gillberry*

The fourth significant variation from the standard LT livery had first appeared in January 1978 and consisted of various shades of green. London Country had no further use for crew-operated vehicles and in October 1977 had begun to sell its Routemasters, both buses and one-time Green Line coaches. Many were in deplorable condition, owing to the crisis in spare parts, and looked to be fit only for scrap, 21 ended their days thus at Wombwell Diesels in Yorkshire. The rest were bought by London Transport. The erstwhile coaches arrived first, many of the RMCs and RCLs going straight onto training duties in January 1978 in green livery, several still retaining London Country fleetnames. The RMLs followed; these being virtually identical to their red relations, they were all overhauled and repainted red and were to serve London for another 20 years or more.

Another source of Routemasters was British Airways, all 65 forward-entrance buses new to British European Airways in 1965/6 passing to London Transport in the years 1975-9 as the RMA class. The first to arrive, most still in latter-day BEA livery of orange and white, ran briefly in service from Romford (North Street) garage on route 175; later acquisitions were used as staff buses, the majority initially in BA blue and white. Finally 12 further forward-entrance Routemasters were acquired from Northern General, in 1979/80, as RMF2761-72. In the event none was used in passenger service, although similar buses hired to LT by dealers appeared on the Round London Sightseeing Tour.

Above: RMA8, one of the initial consignment of 13 ex-British Airways Routemasters used briefly by London Transport on route 175, still in the later orange livery of its original owner, British European Airways. *Gerald Mead*

Below: Three of the BEA Routemasters in the livery they acquired after their operator was merged (in 1973) with the British Overseas Airways Corporation (BOAC) to form British Airways. They are seen lined up in 1975, when the first examples were sold to London Transport.

Above: The 12 Routemasters acquired by LT in 1979/80 from Northern General never made it into service, but earlier FPT 589C, hired to LT as the first RMF2761, was used on sightseeing duties, being seen so employed on the Chelsea Embankment on 29 July 1978. *G. R. Mills*

Below: The 1970s saw an outbreak of overall advertising on Routemasters. RM686, seen here in Charing Cross Road, carried a blue and yellow scheme for Vernon's Pools. *Michael Dryhurst*

• 11 •

Desperate Days for London Country

WHILST London Country was getting rid of its conductors and the buses they worked, the replacement vehicles were proving unreliable. At the same time there was a crisis in spare parts, and a huge number of buses sat around waiting to get back on the road. Our local garages at Chelsham and Godstone became more like graveyards, the former stocked with just about every type of unserviceable bus and coach from RTs to Reliances, whilst Godstone, a garage which had for decades taken a particular pride in the condition of its RTs and RMLs, now presented a depressing sight, with Routemasters parked out the back, paintwork patched and fading, with panels, windows and various other parts missing.

Lincoln-green RCL2228 has found the climb up Sanderstead Hill too much for it, but RMC1515 in NBC leaf green has almost reached the summit. The date is January 1978.

To keep the show on the road a kaleidoscopic array of vehicles was hired in — blue Southend Leyland PD3s and Maidstone Leyland PD2s and Atlanteans, cream Eastbourne AEC Regent Vs, yellow Bournemouth Daimler Fleetlines and Roadliners (bet these were *really* welcomed) and white Royal Blue Bristol MW coaches. One day near East Grinstead I saw approaching me the familiar shape of a Northern Counties-bodied Leyland PD3 in traditional Southdown green and cream. Only this was north rather than south of the Sussex town. For a moment I assumed one of the routes which the south coast company worked into East Grinstead had been extended northwards, only to discover that 6949 CD was on the 409 bound for West Croydon. In its desperation London Country had acquired three of these Titans and sent them to Godstone, where at least one RT was still doing its best to help out on the 409, 410 and 411. These were not the only PD3s to join the London Country fleet, for 20 equally distinctive Burlingham-bodied examples were acquired from Ribble, to be painted yellow and used as trainers.

Above: Two RMCs and an RT at Chelsham in June 1977.

Below: Grays played host to a large number of withdrawn buses, including this RF and a number of Routemasters, seen in front of the gasworks backing on to the garage. How picturesque!

Left: RCL2237 was the very last Routemaster coach to be regularly employed on Green Line duties and the only one to receive Green Line lettering with the National symbol, which it gained upon repainting in March 1975. Despite being used chiefly on the 709 from Godstone, it is seen here bearing an RG (Reigate) code inside Chelsham garage in the spring of 1975!

Above: A far-from-pristine RML pokes its nose into the sun at Garston garage in June 1979. Amongst the assorted buses inside are a National and more Routemasters.

Right: RML2446 climbing Godstone Hill in July 1977. Delivered new to Northfleet, it was transferred late in its London Country career to Godstone, where, it seems, the staff were unable to find it a full set of blinds.

Above: A Massey-bodied Leyland Titan PD3 of Southend Transport (342) on hire to London Country at Harlow, April 1976. *P. J. Snell*

Right: Not the sort of image one expected of a coach service. RP87 carried this all-over Airfix advert for a time in 1973, being seen at Harlow bus station on 19 September. *Bespix*

Below: The desperate straits in which London Country found itself in the late 1970s forced it to hire vehicles from wherever it could. In the spring of 1977 Chelsham received a number of Maidstone Corporation Massey-bodied Leyland Atlanteans, five of which are seen here lined up with an RT and a Routemaster.

Above: Dunton Green in the summer of 1977. Leyland National SNB259, having worked in on the Bromley–Tonbridge 402, stands alongside a demonstration of how desperate London Country had become in its hired-in companion — a Royal Blue Bristol/ECW MW6G coach of 1967, wearing all-white National coach livery.

Below: The full-fronted PD3 was the last fling in the many variations on the Leyland Titan (front-engined version), and, although none ever graced the London Transport fleet, it is perhaps not surprising that London Country, as it struggled to keep the show on the road, acquired two varieties. Taken at the rear of Godstone garage in 1975, this is the only known photograph featuring both types together; it shows one of the three Northern Counties examples acquired from Southdown and used, still in Southdown livery, on the 409 and 411, standing next to one of the ex-Ribble Burlingham-bodied buses of the LR class, which were used as driver trainers. The sorry state of the PD3s, to say nothing of the two RMLs, tells its own story.

Left: LS2, another of the three ex-Southdown Leyland PD3s, still in its former owner's colours, at West Croydon bus station in October 1975.
S. W. Lander

Below: Overhauled RT1018, splendid in NBC leaf green (not something that could be said of many buses so adorned), stands at the Chelsham terminus of the 403 'Express' in the summer of 1977 alongside one of the Burlingham-bodied ex-Ribble Leyland PD3, bought by London Country for training duties.

Bottom: At the other extreme, just about the most miserable-looking RT ever is this hulk, in use as a store at Chelsham in 1977.

Right: An early-morning journey still took the 403 deep into the Surrey countryside to Tatsfield. Here an RCL heads northwards along the ridge of the North Downs in the summer of 1976, past a recently erected stop sign, neither as substantial nor as well designed as the London Transport one it replaced.

Below: By the late 1970s the Routemaster was fast disappearing from the London Country fleet, and by the time this picture was taken at West Croydon in 1979 numbers were down to a handful. The RCLs had already gone, but Chelsham still had a few of the shorter RMCs. From March these were officially restricted to the 403 Express, but in practice they still appeared on the 403 proper, as can be seen from this view of RMC1501 alongside AN184, a recently delivered Roe-bodied Leyland Atlantean.

• 12 •

The Last RFs

IT is perhaps surprising to recall how many London Transport RFs were still crew-operated in 1970, 78 such buses being suitable only for use with conductors. However, within a year all red RFs had been converted to one-man operation. Some 233 were on LT's books in January 1970, although five of these were hired to what had been the Country Area, the last not returning from London Country until March 1971. With huge numbers of new single-deckers entering service the elderly Regal IVs might have been expected to disappear rapidly, but as we have seen, so unreliable were their successors that the much better-engineered RF would be needed, admittedly in steadily decreasing numbers, for most of the decade.

RF491 at the Old Lodge Lane terminus of route 234A just before Croydon lost its last vehicles of this type in January 1977. RF491 would go on to serve as a trainer, a most unusual use for this type of bus.

The BL class of Bristol LHs, which began to enter service in April 1976, accounted for many of the surviving RFs at Romford (North Street), Riverside, Sutton, Fulwell, Enfield, Norbiton, Kingston, Uxbridge, Croydon, Edgware and Hounslow garages. By the spring of 1977 the only RFs still at work were, fittingly, allocated to Kingston, a garage associated with practically every class of single-decker since early General days. Kingston was not just a garage but also a bus station and had long been a Mecca for enthusiasts. No more Bristols were on order, and as these and the RFs were the only single-deckers which could fit over Kingston's inspection pits London Transport decided that 25 RFs had best be reconditioned and given three-year Certificates of Fitness to continue working routes 218 and 219.

RF livery had remained virtually unchanged throughout the class's career in London, the cream beading around the windows giving way to pale grey,

An RF, and SMS, an XA and two RMs
inside Croydon garage at the end of 1976.

the difference not being all that noticeable. However, the 25 refurbished RFs emerged minus the traditional 'LONDON TRANSPORT' fleetname and sporting in its place the white LT roundel. Incidentally the refurbishment was carried out not at Aldenham Works but at Hanwell and Chiswick garages.

At the end of the summer of 1977 I had moved from London Country territory at Oxted to Hants & Dorset territory in Wareham, but I frequently came up to London either by train or by car and could usually be sure of catching a glimpse of the familiar shape of an RF in Esher, Hampton Court or Kingston. Somehow I imagined it would last for ever. Of course, it couldn't.

Reliable to the end and kept in pretty good condition (unlike many of the last RTs), the RF finally retired in the spring of 1979. Reallocated to Norbiton garage, just around the corner from Kingston and with longer inspection pits, the 218/219 could be operated by Leyland Nationals, which took over on 31 March 1979. By this date the enthusiast movement was highly organised, LOTS and Cobham Bus Museum were in business, and London Transport organised the final day with a certain flair. The Mayor and Mayoress of the Royal Borough of Kingston-upon-Thames were presented with one of the famous LT bullseyes from the front of an RF, and the official last scheduled journey was made by a suitably decorated RF507, which had had its 1953 'as delivered' livery restored.

This was not quite the end, for London Country still had just one RF in service, so let us now look at the green version of the class, a colour worn in various shades by the majority. A very large number, 413, was taken over by London Country on 1 January 1970. This was only 37 short of the number originally allocated to Green Line and Country Area bus services when the class first entered service. Although changes to their allocation and working pattern had always taken place and continued through 1970 and into the New Year it was not until the autumn of 1971 that London Country began to dispose of its RFs. Fifteen were put up for sale and soon found buyers. RFs still performed a good deal of Green Line work. Green Line vehicles had never (certainly in London Transport days) been coaches in the true sense of the word, as understood by Southdown, Ribble and such companies, and might more accurately be described as express buses. Thus the modernised RFs were still perfectly adequate for these duties, and London Country decided that its priority was to get rid of its rear-entrance double-deckers, the RTs and Routemasters, which needed conductors.

One Green Line route that did lose its RFs to more modern vehicles was the 711. London Transport

Above: It was fitting that Kingston, a garage with stronger associations with single-deckers than any other within London Transport, should operate the last RFs. This line-up is seen in that most familiar of settings, Kingston bus station, on 19 January 1979.

Below: A typical January day, but the last winter an RF would be seen in ordinary service here; Kingston on 19 January 1979.

Above: RF511, which remained at work until the final day, 30 March 1979, heads through the Esher slush 14 days earlier.

Left: Plenty of snow at Esher, 16 March 1979.

Below: RF522 unloads at Esher on 16 March 1979.

Right: The RF class continued to appear on Green Line duties well into the 1970s. Modernised RF173 is seen at Uxbridge on the 710, 15 July 1971. *M. A. Penn*

Below: RC8 in Stevenage after final demotion of the class from Green Line duty in 1974. These Willowbrook-bodied AEC Reliances of 1965 were a by-word for unreliability, and all had been withdrawn from passenger service by early 1977.

had bought 14 AEC Reliances with 36ft-long Willowbrook bodies, built to BET specification, in 1965. They closely resembled vehicles used by Maidstone & District, which they encountered daily at the Sevenoaks end of the 705 route upon which they worked initially. Sadly they were unreliable and had been delicensed by London Country. In October 1971 they were given an opportunity to redeem themselves and replaced RFs on the 711. Once again they blotted their copybook, and although London Country tried its best, first on other Green Line services then on bus routes from Hertford, by 1977 they had ceased passenger service, and by 1979 all had passed to the scrapman. Later Reliances proved

to be a much better investment, and many coach firms preferred them to the Leyland Leopard.

As the 1970s wore on the London Country RFs, once so well maintained and of standardised appearance, began to look sadder and shabbier and became a real ragbag collection of misfits. They were sent to perform a variety of duties at a variety of garages, still being more reliable than most more modern vehicles. To deal with the extended destination blinds details were reduced, with the top and bottom of the screens blanked off so that in many cases only the destination and route number were shown, which had not been the London Transport way of doing things. There were even examples of blinds which

read 'LINE GREEN' rather than 'GREEN LINE', and others wore nothing other than a chalked route number. As for liveries . . . well, just about every shade of green known to man and nature could, by the mid-1970s, be found on the RF class — often, it seemed, on a single vehicle, where the paintwork was fading and had been patched up. Bright yellow, then white was used to relieve the green, but in other instances there was no relief at all. I took a picture of an RF, painted National green all over, standing amongst the slush outside Oxted station in

Below: RF684 was the last surviving London Country RF built as a bus and the last in traditional Lincoln green. It is seen here at Limpsfield Chart shortly before withdrawal in May 1978.

Above: In early 1977 RF684, the last RF still wearing traditional Lincoln green, stands outside Oxted station as a lady alights, taking care not to disturb BN37.

January 1975, and a drabber, sadder sight was hard to imagine.

Our RFs worked in from East Grinstead and Chelsham garages; RMLs and an occasional RT came from Godstone, the one and only London Country garage which in 1970 had no RFs allocated. East Grinstead worked the 494, a deeply rural route which would soon disappear, Chelsham the 464 and 465, once the preserve of GSs. These had a more assured future, serving, as they did, the various

Left: RF221, by now repainted in NBC leaf green, still on Green Line duty in September 1977. *G. Brigden*

Below: A remarkable number of RFs have been preserved. During the summer of 1978 RF429 paid a visit to Dorset, being seen in North Street, Wareham, approaching the ancient Saxon church which contains Eric Kennington's famous carved effigy of Lawrence of Arabia, who died nearby in a motorcycle accident in 1935.

housing estates in and around Oxted, as well as the surrounding countryside and terminating in Holland, which was not beside the Zuider Zee but a hamlet south of Oxted. Some of these estates were of council houses but were in the process of being sold off, fetching high prices, for they were in excellent condition, often semi-detached with large gardens, and were snapped up by office workers or, as they preferred to be known, young executives, working in tower-block offices in Croydon or London, which were within easy reach by train.

The very last RF in original bus form was Chelsham's RF684. Still in Lincoln green, it was a regular in and around Oxted until delicensed in May 1978. Even longer-lived was RF221, which had begun its London career at Chelsham and was destined to end it there 27 years later. It had been recertified in June 1977 and repainted in full corporate livery, with the red and blue National

'double-N' symbol on a white background, which suited it rather well. It finished work in October 1978. Last of all was RF202. This was a modernised coach and retained the Green Line fleetname on NBC livery. Working from Northfleet garage, it was allocated both bus and Green Line duties, the latter on routes 725 and 726. A faulty gearbox finally ended its London career — and thus that of the entire RF class — in July 1979, four months after the last red RF had ceased work. No ceremony accompanied RF202's demise, although this was only temporary, for it was preserved by its owners and is still in existence, albeit with several changes of registration; its current one is MLL 528, and it lives far to the south-west of its original home, in Lostwithiel, Cornwall. A quite extraordinary number of RFs has been preserved, around 100 at the last count, so they are still a familiar sight at rallies, museums and operating special services.

· 13 ·

The Last Green RTs

THE newest RT in the London Country fleet on 1 January 1970 was 16 years old, although there were some (with OLD registrations) which had been placed in store upon delivery and had not entered service until 1958. Mechanically all 484 were still sound and so was their bodywork, but the fact that they needed a two-man crew doomed them to early extinction. At least, that was the intention, but they were not so easily put down, and in practice the RT almost saw out the decade. Indeed, although passenger service ended in September 1978 there were still two in use as trainers in 1980.

Knowing that they would have to soldier on for a while, London Country arranged for 56 RTs to be overhauled under contract by London Transport at Aldenham Works between early 1971 and the spring of 1972, whilst others were attended to at London Country garages. Still others had to settle for just a repaint, some still in the traditional Lincoln green with garish yellow additions, but later repaints were in a paler, rather more attractive green. Whilst this was going on many less fortunate members of the class were falling by the wayside, more than 100 being

withdrawn in 1971. Even more disappeared the following year, so that by New Year's Day 1973 fewer than 100 RTs were licensed for service. Among the disposals were 34 bought back by London Transport. Repainted red, they saw further service, RT3251/4 surviving to the very end at Barking garage on 7 April 1979.

There was something of a lull in the decline of the RT through 1973 and 1974 and for the first six months of 1975. Then up in the north trunk routes 301/2, as well as several local routes based on Tring and Hemel Hempstead, were lost. By this date two learner RTs, RT2230 and 2367, had donned NBC green livery, but neither ever carried passengers in this condition.

Chelsham, being one of my local garages, had always been kept under close scrutiny. For decades I had thought myself practically the only enthusiast thereabouts, but by early 1976 it had become popular with the camera-toting fraternity, as most of London Country's still active RTs, as well as a number of dead ones, could be found there.

By April 1977 the 403, along with Luton's 360, was the only route with an official allocation of RTs, although they continued to pop up elsewhere. They disappeared from Luton in September 1976, Luton garage itself not lasting much longer; it was always a rather curious situation that London's green buses should share Luton's streets with the municipality's own buses, and in November 1976 the London Country garage passed to United Counties, being closed soon afterwards.

I was standing at the 410 stop by Redhill station in April 1977, having just returned from accepting a teaching post in Dorset which meant, of course, that later that year the family would up sticks and leave London Country

Newly repainted RT1018 climbs
Sanderstead Hill in the spring of 1977.

behind when, not the expected AF hove into view, but what for a moment I assumed must be a preserved RT done up in an unaccustomed livery. It was RT1018 and, although a dull day, it positively gleamed in full bright leaf green with grey wheels and the 'double-N' logo. Harsh things have been said about the insensitive, all-embracing NBC livery which superseded so many more attractive schemes, but in its defence I don't think any RT ever looked as good as did RT1018 that April day. It had been repainted at Northfleet and must have visited headquarters at Reigate before heading for Chelsham, for that is where it was bound. In the next two months two more RTs in the same attractive livery, RT3461 and RT604, joined it at Chelsham, where they worked on the 403 and the 453, alongside Routemasters and borrowed Maidstone Borough Council Leyland Atlanteans. As they arrived at roughly monthly intervals we wondered if this phœnix-like revival would continue on and on, but sadly that was it.

This Indian summer was short-lived, for by September 1977 RT1018 and RT3461 were relegated to training duties, still at Chelsham. However, RT604, ostensibly no less than 30 years old and probably the most photographed RT of all time, kept going to the year's end and beyond, its engine finally giving up the ghost in June 1978. For some weeks it sat behind the garage with a gaping hole where the engine should have been, and we all hoped that a replacement would be fitted. It was not to be. Eventually it was sold in July 1979, but such a celebrity could hardly be passed to the scrapman. Instead a replacement engine was obtained, and RT604 lives on — fittingly in its final livery and equally fittingly close to where it passed its final working days — in the care of the Purley Preservation Group.

Above: A Triumph Dolomite and RT1018 (again) at the head of a line of DMSs at West Croydon bus station in June 1977.

Left: RT1018 and RMC1473 at Chelsham in July 1977. The RT has the more up-to-date National symbol.

Above: Chelsham's RT3461, in NBC leaf green, heads north through outer suburbia during the summer of 1977. *L. D. S. Dolan*

Below: RT981 in service as a driver trainer at St Albans c1979. *Kevin Lane*

• **14** •

The Last Red RTs

ALTHOUGH the RT fleet of 1 January 1970 was much diminished from its zenith of 1954, there were still 2,775 RTs scheduled for peak-time service, a huge number by any standards. The Leylands had almost all gone, a few RTLs remaining as staff buses, a few RTWs as trainers. The very last roofbox RT10 finished work on the 109 from Thornton Heath garage on 9 February 1970. Some roofbox Saunders examples survived the year — just — but all of these had gone by January 1971.

Merton's RT4459, with a piece of cardboard protecting its radiator from the cold winter winds, heads through South Norwood shortly before the last roofbox RTs finished passenger service with London Transport in early 1971.

London Transport claimed that putting the number indicator high up weakened the roof structure, but this seems doubtful, no preserved bus with this feature showing any such evidence. Whatever the reason, although it had been around since the 1920s, it would be seen no more; a roofbox Routemaster might have been rather fetching, and how about one — or a whole fleet — of the modern generation of low-floor double-deckers so equipped?

Unlike the situation that would apply during the latter days of the Routemaster, LT policy in the 1970s was to remove the RT from Central London and confine it largely to the suburbs. Sadly, as the decade wore on, many members of what might reasonably be claimed was the finest and best-appointed half-cab double-deck class ever built fell into disrepair. One

RT4771 of Catford garage and AN25 of Leatherhead at West Croydon in March 1977.

route upon which I regularly travelled was the 109, one of the last to serve Central London, and inside and out some of both the Brixton and Thornton Heath allocations were in a sorry state, with bare metal showing in places around the roofs and patched and sometimes torn upholstery inside.

Overhaul of RTs ceased in 1970, but repainting continued, and in 1972 a number were recertified, thereby gaining another three years' service. It had been expected that the last RT would be withdrawn by 1975, but such was the state of their replacements — Merlins, Swifts and Fleetlines — that there would clearly be work for the RT class for several more years, so recertifications, both three- and one-year, resumed. So dire was the situation that several RT trainers were recertified for passenger service.

The 109 kept its RTs until the autumn of 1976, Routemasters eventually replacing them. By the beginning of 1977 RTs were officially only to be seen in Central London on the 155, and this was converted to RM on 10 January. However, the class still made its presence felt, filling in for more modern types from a number of garages which served the City and the West End, whilst until the middle of 1978 seven Barking-based RTs were required at night to work the N95 and N98 to and from Victoria.

Numbers were now down to the low hundreds, 236 being scheduled for service at the beginning of 1978. April of that year saw the end of RTs in my home town, Croydon, when Catford withdrew them from the 54. Croydon was the very last place on the LT network where red and green RTs could be seen alongside each other, for Chelsham's RT604, re-painted in NBC green, regularly passed Catford RTs drawn up at the Fairfield Halls terminus of the 54. Rather surprisingly RTs, many of them very careworn, continued to appear at Heathrow, the world's busiest airport, until they bowed out of the 140, worked by Harrow Weald garage, in July 1978.

The year 1979 opened with just 13 RTs available for passenger service. These were for route 62, which ran from Barking to Barkingside and was worked by Barking garage. The last-but-one RT route had been the 87, also worked by Barking, on which the type had been replaced on 28 October 1978. Barking is, I'm sure, a very nice place but not one that had until then featured prominently in holiday brochures. Suddenly, from the summer of 1978, any householder

Above: The last place where red and green RTs could be seen together in ordinary passenger service was Croydon. Chelsham's RT1018 leads Catford's RT840 at West Croydon bus station in the summer of 1977.

Below: Croydon's last red RT route, the 54, succumbed on 22 April 1978. Three RTs, headed by RT2292 and RT1088, stand at the Croydon terminus whilst a Chelsham RMC passes on the other side of the road in the summer of 1977.

Above: Bexleyheath also lost its RTs, from route 89, in April 1978. Here RT4595 heads for (Le)wisham shortly before the end.

Below: At the start of 1978 Palmers Green still managed to hang on to a few RTs, which worked the 261. RT3928 is seen at Arnos Grove Station shortly before RMs took over, briefly, in April 1978, prior to giving way to DMSs.

By October 1978 RTs were operating just two LT routes, both from Barking garage. The penultimate one was the 87. RT2773 negotiates Barking town centre on 27 October 1978, the last day of RT operation.

living in the district with a room or two to spare could have made a good few bob taking in paying guests, as enthusiasts — no doubt the locals thought them 'barking' mad — flocked in, not just from all over the London area but from far beyond, to record the last days in service of the RT.

Saturday 7 April 1979 saw the RT finally cease regular scheduled service in London. Whilst the gradual withdrawal of the RT had not been marked route by route with the grand gestures which would accompany Routemaster retirements 26 years later, the stops were certainly pulled out at the very end. As the posters displayed on the final 12 RTs proclaimed, it was the end of 40 years' service to the capital and its suburbs — although, of course, no individual bus had served that long.

So we all took ourselves off to Barking, to the less-than-utter delight of some of the residents in the flats opposite the garage, but their balconies were too good a grandstand to ignore. The last 62 journey was scheduled to arrive back at the garage at around lunchtime. The bus chosen was RT624, nominally the oldest, the original 624 being a green Weymann-bodied roofbox RT3 delivered to Hemel Hempstead garage in August 1948, more than 30 years earlier. Following this a grand cavalcade was staged of all

the serviceable Barking RTs and various other preserved examples. The star was RT1. OK, not *all* of it was the original daddy of them all, but then none of the others was what it purported to be. Surprisingly no 'prewar' RT had joined the London Transport collection, although several had been preserved privately.

The unassuming-sounding 1037J was an engineering unit which had been in the service fleet since 1956 and was to serve 22 years in this form. Certain specialised engineering-fleet vehicles have had long lives, but 22 years was exceptional by any standards. The chassis was from Cravens-bodied RT1420, and the body — and this is where you need to hold your breath — was none other than that fitted in March 1939 to chassis No O661.6749 to form RT1. Preservationists were aware of its existence, and eventually, in 1978, it was sold. Tim Nicholson, Principal Engineer involved in the restoration of the much older D142 and ST922, was very keen that

Left: And so we come to 7 April 1979, when the RT finally finished normal passenger service with London Transport. Large crowds of enthusiasts turned up to witness the event, and LT played its part, as did the police, although this was one of their less arduous duties. Cameras ready, these photographers are probably not too interested in getting either the policemen or the DMS in their pictures.

Below: Yet other photographers ascended to the balconies on the block of flats opposite Barking garage, being not altogether welcomed by the residents.

Above: Inside the garage RT624, officially LT's last passenger-carrying RT, prepares for the final parade.

Left: The star of the show, RT1, its paintwork scarcely dry, joins the parade, its distinctive rear, with roof-mounted number box, illustrating one of the chief variations from the postwar RT.

most others, I had no idea what was going on behind the scenes. I was standing by the front of the cavalcade beside Barking garage when the glorious and totally unexpected sight of RT1, complete with original registration EYK 396, hove into view, pursued by clicking shutters, and proudly took its rightful place at the head of the cavalcade.

Sadly Prince Marshall, who had done so much towards the London bus-preservation scene, died two years later, and RT1 was bought and shipped out to the USA. This was a tragedy, but thank goodness Michael Dryhurst, a name as familiar to the preservation movement and public-transport literature as Prince, and who was living in California, was instrumental in getting it brought back to the UK in 1986. It put in a number of appearances at rallies before undergoing an extensive restoration, which is ongoing as I write.

Which brings us to the London Bus Preservation Trust. I write this a week after spending a day riding around part of the very last RM route, the 159, aboard ST922, a former Thomas Tilling AEC Regent of 1930, which Prince Marshall saved for preservation after it had spent several years in a scrapyard. It now lives at Cobham Bus Museum in the safe hands of

Prince Marshall buy RT1, which he did. Now there were just six months left to get it ready to take part in the Barking cavalcade. The bus was towed to LPC Coachworks in Hounslow and work began.

One issue involved the livery. RT1 had worn a number of variations in its early days, and it was decided to go back to its very first when it had been displayed to the press and public in the spring of 1939 with white window surrounds, silver roof and with blinds for route 164A, although it had never actually worked this. The full story of all that had to be done, both mechanically and to the body, is recounted in *The First RTs* by Alan Townsin and Tony Beard, published by Capital Transport in 1996.

The paint was not quite dry on the evening of 6 April, but RT1 made it the following morning. Like the LBPT. I had last ridden it in Central London back in 1972, when it had worked heritage route 100. The LBPT moved into an old aircraft factory once owned by the Vickers group in the spring of 1972. Its founder member, the late, much-missed Bill Cottrell, recalled: 'I had a quarter share in Q83, a 1935 Q-type single-deck country bus . . . our group realised that under-cover accommodation was a priority'. Before they were able to move in, 'there was a tense month to wait, and the time was used to . . . clean up the accumulated debris left by the previous occupants. These ranged from a heavy-engineering company repairing lifts to a country retreat for gentlemen of the road.' Today the LBPT, which plans to move into splendid new premises in the Brooklands complex, is home to a wonderful collection of London buses and coaches ranging from pre-London Transport days to the post-Chiswick-design era. Its buses can be seen out and about, bringing reminders of days past to the general public as well as the enthusiast fraternity, whilst its annual Easter-time rally attracts hundreds of vehicles and thousands of visitors.

Above: For a time in the early 1970s preserved Thomas Tilling ST922 worked vintage service 100 through Central London, being seen here in Trafalgar Square in the summer of 1972.

Below: In 1974 the London Bus Preservation Trust held its first open day at its Cobham headquarters, and this soon became one of the principal events in the bus-preservation calendar. This is a photograph taken two years later in a building erected during World War 2 for the production of aircraft components.

· 15 ·

The Underground Expands

JULY 1971 saw the opening of the final section of the first completely new Tube line since Edwardian times. The Victoria Line had been in the planning stage for decades, the necessity of an underground route to provide quicker, direct travel from the area around the Thames at Pimlico, through Victoria and the West End to Euston, King's Cross and the Walthamstow direction having long been recognised. As one might expect, many advances in technology were employed, the one the press lighted on being that it was 'driverless'. That was its description, but it was only partially correct — there's a surprise! Automatic Train Operation, which had been tried out on sections of the Underground system in the 1960s, meant that starting and stopping of Victoria Line trains were controlled automatically, the person in the cab having responsibility for door operation and signalling that the train was ready to start. London south of the Thames had been — indeed, still is — poorly served by the Underground, and the extension to Pimlico, Vauxhall, Stockwell and Brixton was a significant advance in what was almost virgin territory.

The next landmark in the extension of the system was the opening of the Piccadilly Line to Heathrow in December 1977; it seems extraordinary now that the world's busiest airport should until then have been only accessible by road. Diving below ground after a long stretch in the open air, the trains reached Terminals 1, 2 and 3 in the heart of what had by this date become a fair-sized town. A further extension in the 1980s would bring them below Terminal 4. Costing £71 million, the Heathrow extension enabled passengers to reach Central London in 40 minutes. Travelling by Tube train serving a series of suburban stations between the airport and central London was not the perfect answer for the air traveller: that would have to wait for the Heathrow Express to/from Paddington, although there would still be a need for the obvious surface-line connection via the Southern's Hounslow line and Waterloo.

London Transport issued a statement that, although each train had 64 spaces, 'big enough for two cases . . . travellers are warned not to use the service if they cannot manage their luggage alone on the Tube'. The Queen, recalling that her great-grandfather, King Edward VII, had opened the original 'Tuppenny Tube' in 1890, performed the unveiling ceremony and wished 'success to those who manage the line and those who will travel on it'. The fare was 80p, which compared with £1 by airport bus and £5.50 (plus tip, as we were tartly informed) by taxi.

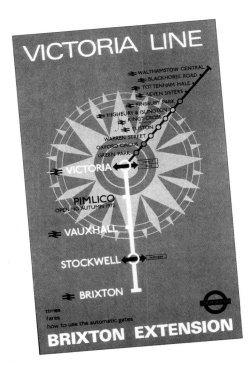

Victoria Line Brixton-extension pamphlet dating from the summer of 1971.

Above: The ceremonial opening of the Piccadilly Line's Heathrow extension was performed by the Queen on 16 December 1977. *London Transport*

Below: A train of 1973 stock arrives at Heathrow Central station in 1978. *John Glover*

· 16 ·

Yet More Underground Progress

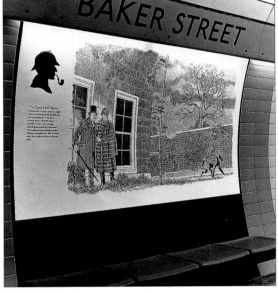

THE year 1979 was a very good one down below. A new Tube line, the Jubilee, opened, whilst nearer the surface the District Line was equipped with the latest rolling stock, 450 cars, classified 'D'.

To be truthful the Jubilee Line wasn't *that* new. Most of it consisted of the old Bakerloo Line, from Baker Street to Stanmore; what *was* new was the section most people noticed and the most heavily used, the two and a half miles from Baker Street by way of Bond Street and Green Park to Charing Cross. It should have been completed two years earlier, hence its title, and there was supposed to be much more. Eventually it would reach Stratford by way of some magnificent stations, quite the equal of anything erected in the great days of the 1930s, but this would not happen until 1999.

Right: The Jubilee Line platforms at Baker Street station featured scenes from the 'Sherlock Holmes' novels.

Below: Green Park station layout. *Both London Transport*

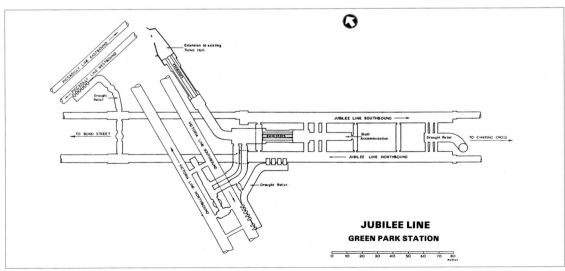

JUBILEE LINE
GREEN PARK STATION

Above: A train of 1972 stock arriving at Stanmore station on the Jubilee Line. *John Glover*

The 'D' stock was similar in appearance to the 'C' stock. Each car had four doors on each side, the cars, at around 60ft, being longer than their predecessors, built to metric measurements, so that a six-car train of 'D' stock was able to replace a seven-car formation of 'CO'/'CP' or 'R' stock. A good deal of the technology used in the 'D' stock was similar to that in the 1973 Tube stock, motors and wheels and a fault-finding Train Equipment Panel. The first six-car unit arrived from Metro-Cammell in June 1979, but none actually entered passenger service until the first month of 1980. There would eventually be 75 trains and a total of 450 cars. Livery was the now standard aluminium but with a red panel below the cab on the front of each unit.

Right: A train of 'D' stock leaving Richmond for Upminster. The dealer's yard in the background is host to a large number of ex-London Transport buses, mostly from the RT family but also including a lone AEC Swift. *John Glover*

· 17 ·

The Clouds Begin to Roll Away

AFTER the disasters of the Merlins, Swifts and DMSs the introduction of the MD class in March 1976 promised better things. I first came across examples on the 36, a route I had travelled since a very small child. This would bring us from Victoria to Paddington, where we would alight and board a Great Western Railway express, to be hauled, towering over minuscule-looking Tube trains, through the Chilterns, the rich farmlands of Buckinghamshire, Northamptonshire and Warwickshire, on to Birmingham and deep into the industrial Midlands, by a 'King' 4-6-0 steam locomotive, if not actually designed by God then by someone who had a pretty good idea of his preferences. Thus I was

Below: One of the stylish Scania/MCW Metropolitans, MD43, heads through Peckham on route 36 in the summer of 1976. *M. S. Curtis*

favourably disposed towards the 36, and the Scania BR111DH-based MCW Metropolitan MDs which Peckham garage put in service on this route did not disappoint. The MD bore a strong resemblance to the DMS but had an asymmetrical windscreen, a rather racy aluminium strip below the lower deck windows and white upper-deck window surrounds. Much quieter than the DMS, it had real style. Problems arose later with the bodywork, and, being non-standard, the class had a short life in London, the majority being withdrawn between the autumn of 1982 and the following summer.

The MD was certainly not regarded as a failure, and it led to a new standard class which would eventually number 1,485 units and serve London for more than 25 years. This was the M. Contemporary with the Ms were the Ts, also introduced in 1978, a class which would total 1,131 buses and would last virtually as long as the Ms.

The M — for Metrobus —was designed and built solely by MCW in Birmingham. London bought the greatest number, followed, not surprisingly, by West Midlands PTE. A demonstrator was inspected in December 1977, and London's first five examples arrived in 1978 and took up work from Cricklewood garage on the 16/16A, working initially with conductors. Visually the bodywork of the M was similar to that of the DMS, although the M had the asymmetrical windscreen of the MD, and the earliest deliveries had white upper-deck window surrounds. They had Gardner 6LXB engines. An initial production batch of 200 was ordered for delivery in 1978/9, modifications on these including a revised indicator display and the loss (from M56) of the

Above: London Transport's first Metrobuses perpetuated the attractive livery with white upper-deck window surrounds introduced as standard on the Metropolitans and later Fleetlines. M13, a Fulwell vehicle, passes through Teddington in May 1979.

Below: On later Metrobuses the white relief was abandoned. M66, a Norbiton bus, is seen at Hampton Court when new in May 1979.

white window surrounds. The type, particularly the early examples, was very much associated with the western area of the London Transport empire, Kingston, Richmond, Harlesden, Acton and Ealing, for example, being happy hunting-grounds.

The T was a Leyland bus, T standing for Titan, a revival of a greatly revered name. By the mid-1970s the name of Leyland itself had suffered greatly, being almost a synonym for poor design and general incompetence, but thankfully the Titan did not further besmirch it. Well before the last DM had entered service (and when it had become obvious that the rear-engined Routemaster would never go into production) British Leyland and London Transport engineers began to work together to produce a double-decker which would not only suit the arduous London conditions but which would also sell elsewhere. In this they were only partly successful: the B15, as it was initially code-named, did indeed prove to be an excellent London bus, but for the rest it was deemed a bit too sophisticated and, crucially, expensive. It *did*, eventually, sell elsewhere, for when the time came for the type to be phased out

in London it was snapped up, like the RT and the Routemaster families before it, proving to be an excellent second-hand bargain.

Your average passenger would not have seen much advance in the Titan's interior appointments. When I climbed aboard one of the prototypes on display at a Cobham open day and pointed out to my five-year-old son that he was now aboard the bus of the future he said: 'What's so new about this, Daddy?' But what was new about the Titan was that, first of all, it was reliable, secondly that it was popular with passengers. To quote *Commercial Motor*, 'Not only is the quality of ride — particularly on the upper deck — of the B15 superb, but noise and vibration are virtually absent'.

As with the M, the standard engine on the T class was the Gardner 6LXB. After two prototypes had worked on route 24, the first production buses were sent to Hornchurch garage in December 1978, and, just as the Ms were associated with West London, so the Ts were with the East, although latterly this pattern became much less clear-cut. Bodywork was by Park Royal. This firm, of course, had long been associated with London Transport, building, along with Weymann, more bodies for London buses than any other. But by the 1970s it was, like AEC (which ceased production in May 1979) just down the road at Southall, in decline, labour relations being just one of its troubles, and in 1979 came the announcement that the factory was to close. It managed to complete the first 250 Ts, but later examples came from the Leyland factory at Workington. Not, perhaps, as well-proportioned as the M, with unusually large lower-deck windows and an odd, asymmetrical rear aspect, the Titan nevertheless proved ideal for London conditions and would last into the 21st century.

The Reliances did much to give Green Line a better public image, which had been brought to a pretty low level by the Leyland National, and more would be bought until the type ceased production in 1979.

By the end of the 1970s London Transport was beginning to recover from the disaster days of the Merlin *débâcle* and the scarcely better DMS saga. There would be no more AECs, and the RT and the RF were gone from passenger service, but the Routemaster seemed to have an assured future. Whatever was happening in the rest of the country, one-person-operation was not seen as practical on the most heavily used Central London routes. The purpose-built Leyland Titan and MCW Metrobus were proving satisfactorily reliable for all other double-deck needs, while the Leyland National was the preferred single-decker.

The year 1977 saw the introduction of the first true coaches for Green Line duties since the early 1930s. Thirty of them, based on the AEC Reliance chassis, which had by now overcome its earlier problems and was proving popular, took up work. Fifteen had Plaxton Supreme bodywork, the other 15 the not dissimilar Duple Dominant II. Both coach-builders were based in seaside resorts, Plaxton at Scarborough, Duple in Blackpool, a singularly appropriate situation for builders of coach bodies. Duple had for many years been based at Hendon, in North London, but, like Park Royal and Weymann, was finding it difficult to recruit and hold on to workers; its Blackpool factory had originally belonged to Burlingham, builder of the highly successful Seagull coach body of the 1950s and double-deck bus bodywork much favoured by Ribble.

Ten years on from its creation London Country's showed little evidence of its London Transport origins. The conductor had just about vanished, and the Leyland National was to be seen everywhere from East Grinstead to High Wycombe, being barely distinguishable from its fellows belonging to Southdown, Maidstone & District, Eastern National and United Counties. For the time being the former Country Area of the London Transport network remained more or less intact, but many wondered how long this would last. Just as they wondered how the troubles ailing the once-mighty British Leyland would come to affect the London scene.

Below: Two Green Line Duple-bodied AEC Reliance coaches at Windsor in 1979 — RB50 (left) dating from 1977, RB85 (right) from 1978.

Bibliography

Books

abc London Transport Buses (various editions),
  Ian Allan Publishing

London Transport Bus Garages by John Aldridge,
  Ian Allan Publishing (2001)

An Illustrated History of London Buses by Kevin Lane,
  Ian Allan Publishing (1997)

London Transport Buses (various editions) by Lawrie Bowles,
  Capital Transport (1977-80)

London Country Buses and Green Line Coaches
  (various editions) by Mark Chapman,
  Capital Transport (1977-79)

Reshaping London's Buses by Barry Arnold and
  Mike Harris, Capital Transport (1982)

RT by Ken Blacker, Capital Transport (1984)

RF by Ken Glazier, Capital Transport (1991)

The Routemaster Bus by Colin Curtis, Midas Books (1981)

Routemaster, Volume 1 by Ken Blacker, Capital Transport
  (1991)

Routemaster, Volume 2 by Ken Blacker, Capital Transport
  (1992)

Steam to Silver by J. Graeme Bruce, Capital Transport
  (1983)

Periodicals

London Bus Magazine (various editions), LOTS

Cobham Bus Museum Magazine (various editions),
  edited by Bill Cottrell

Various local and national newspapers

Various local timetables, maps and guides

A highly varied collection on display at Cobham Bus Museum. From left to right are 'sit-up-and-beg' STL441, repatriated from Belgium, prototype Leyland-engined Routemaster RML3, 1954 prototype Leyland Atlantean XTC 684 — not looking at all like the production bus but bearing a distinct similarity to the Green Line TF coach of 1939 — and prototype Leyland Titan (B15) BCK 706R — forerunner of a standard London type of the 1980s.